THE WAR OF PRINCIPALITIES

THE WAR OF PRINCIPALITIES

DEAN C. GARDNER

Ordering Information:

For orders and inquiries, please contact:
1-888-404-1388
www.goldtouchpress.com
book.orders@goldtouchpress.com

Printed in the United States of America

Contents

In memory of Nam Jin,
my precious second wife.

SECTION 1

Carrying a load

So
The puppet masters launched
Germ warfare upon the world
But Lady Liberty and the free spirits
Did not flinch.

It was
A fight for freedom
That brought the hammer down
Striking a chord in the heart
Of Lady Liberty
As she geared up for battle.

There was
No turning back
As she approached the front lines
And the children of promise
Steadied aim
At the puppet masters.

Battling against mind control
The free spirits engaged
The adversary with Truth
And The Spirit of Wisdom
Drove time and space
As the engine
Of The Unknown God.

Then
Lady Liberty mounted
The canons
Of the always already there
Signaling the rise
Of what matters
And the world trembled
With anticipation.

So
It was a new
Cold war facing the land
Of the free and the brave
And there were
Puppet masters throughout
The here and now.

How
Power drugged
Minds of contempt
And they fostered
The rhetoric of deception.

So
Power feeds on power
With the appetite
For more power
Never satisfied.

It was
All or nothing in the war
Of principalities.

So
The puppet masters wanted
To rule the world
In a time
When domestic tranquility
Was at a low
And Lady Liberty
Was put in jeopardy.

It was
A time when Lock N. Load
Assembled
The children of promise
Into patriots of the land
Of the free and brave.

How
The households
Across the land
Armed themselves
Against hatred
As they filled their arsenal
Of love
To fight the good fight.

It was
A time when the cities
Counted the dead
In multitudes
Because gangs clogged
The cities with carnage.

So
There was chaos domestically
And threats internationally

As the patriots prepared
To defend civil liberties
And they were ready, willing, and able
To face death with the life of freedom.

It was
A time when an old man
Took the mantle of prayer
To The Unknown God
For deliverance
To regain life, liberty
And the pursuit of happiness.

How
Strong the determination
Of the patriots
When equipped
With the true spirit
The Word.

So
The unknown walked
Into the now
Unsettling the destiny
Of a nation and world.

So
An old man communed
With The Unknown God
As the patriots listened
To the way, the Truth
And the life.

There is
A channel to the beyond
A passageway to pure music
An unearthing of possibility
As mind travels
Through the unknown
Guided by the light
Of forevermore.

How
Time present allows
The heart to feel
The deep touch
And to leap
Into the wonders
Of The Unknown God.

So
Eternity begins
In the here and now
As thoughts probe
Things in themselves
As meditation sees
Through the looking glass
Of Truth
As faith in The Word
Speaks the language
Of the always already there.

It is
The clarity of the authentic article
And the grace of blessed assurance
That allow being toward Truth
To liberate self

As the will to be
Drives passion into the moment.

The
The physics of times and a half
Trumpets the existential moment
And being and nothingness
Listens to the way
The Truth and the life.

Then
The shadows of the dull round
Fall into silence
As pure music exacts
The rhythm of hope
And being toward Truth rides
Into the dawn of the everlasting.

Then
Time present rolls
Into a parabola of time
As an anthem
Of liberty carries life
Into abundance.

So
To be with the authentic article
And to dwell
With blessed assurance
Encompasses all and everything.

So
Truth speaks with a clear mind
And a pure heart.

It was
The madness
Of a lethal virus
That snatched reason
As mind floundered
In the shadows of nothingness.

So
A moment beyond time
Saturated being toward Truth
With the signals
Of hidden meaning, indecipherable
And penetrating.

Then
A barrage of thought
Led no where
But encompassed
The here and now
With trepidation.

So
It was that
The puppet masters
Unleashed a virus
To compromise a world
And the dull world sunk
Into trembling.

Their plan
Was to weaken mankind
And nations of Truth
To enable their tyranny
To take control
Over global concerns.

So
A world took
To The Unknown God
In prayer
Seeking refuge
From the plague.

How
Faith in The Word
Strengthened the afflicted
And nation after nation
Cleared a vision to victory

Then
The deep touch reached
Into the interstices of mind
And bones shook violently
Until the breath of Truth
Opened the living to life.

Soon
The puppet masters shall fall.

Vengeance by The Unknown God
Is swift and complete.

Transfixing his trance
On The Word
Lock N. Load climbed
Out of self
Traveling through mind
Into the chasm
Between being and nothingness.

There was
An echo of Truth
In the wind
As he reached into a portal
Revealing the majesty
Of The Unknown God.

Suddenly
Time and space collapsed
And the rise
Of The Spirit of Wisdom
Embraced being toward Truth.

It was
The workings of eternity
That brought the way
The Truth and the life
Into focus
As Olivia from oblivion
Opened the door
To the other side
Of the sky.

So
The mystery of life
Centered
Upon faith and not thought
As trumpets followed
Olivia
Into the heart of Lock N. Load.

It was
The sound of pure music
That configured the moment
And the rhythm

Of the unknown
Loosened the tongue
Of hidden meaning.

Then
The wind carried
A message of Truth
And Olivia from oblivion
Awoke the bones
Of Lock N. Load
As he saw the trace
Of the everlasting
In the looking glass.

So
Lock N. Load traveled
Into the deep touch.

On the road
With The Unknown God
Time and space phased
Into a parabola of time
As Lock N. Load
Pulled being toward Truth
Into trance.

There was
The dance of Olivia
From oblivion
On the horizon
Where the servants
Of The Word
Emanated pure music.

They were known
As the children of promise
And soldiers of Truth.

It was
A time of war
Against the puppet masters
As Lock N. Load patrolled
The backlands of mind
And as far as he could tell
He was not subject
To their thought control.

In the darkness
Of want
His faith delivered him
To the light
Of the everlasting
As his meditation
Purged him of infamy.

He was
There to preserve
And protect
The little earthlings
From the abys
That the puppet masters
Taught
As the way to be.

How
Olivia from oblivion
Was the destination
Of his heart.

How
His companions
The children of promise
Fought the good fight
For freedom
Against the oppressors
Those consumed by the want
For control.

Endless
The road took him
Into the substance
Of what matters.

So
The plague unleashed
By the puppet masters
Spread across the globe
With death
As the way of its path.

It was
A time when life
Crumbled beneath the weight
Of this pestilence
And the puppet masters
Readied for their claim
As rulers of the world.

How
Sinister this plot
To devour a planet.

How
Hungry for power
These puppet masters.

There was
No Truth in them
As they ate life
Out of the living
As the dirge of death
Marched across the planet.

So
It was germ warfare
On a global scale
And the world raced
Toward hope
With the faith
In The Unknown God.

Lock N. Load
Saw devastation
While in trance
And he heard the cries
Of the afflicted.

Then
Time and times
And a half passed
And the dead
Filled the streets
Their decay a testament
To corrupt minds.

How
Dark the hearts
Of the puppet masters.

So
Now the spirits
Of the dead
Haunt the puppet masters
Tormenting them
With the voice
Of retribution.

Then
Lock N. Load pursued
The deep touch
While in trance
As he entered
A parabola of time.

There was
An image of a stallion
In gold
Its mane a stark white
And its symmetry
Of lean muscle
Powerful in its stride.

Speaking of trepidation
The sky embraced
Being toward Truth
With a rare patch of blue
And the landscape
Dressed the mood
In shades of umber.

Then
In a moment

A lion leaped
Upon the stallion's back
And the struggle began.

It was
Brute strength
Pitted against a life
Of freedom
As the stallion fought
The lion.

Then
The image faded
Into time and space
As the rain came heavy.

Suddenly
Nothingness appeared
As Lock N. Load looked
Into the mirror of life
And Olivia from oblivion
Stood at the threshold
Of the beyond.

There was
The taste of death
To the moment.

So
The vision wrote itself
Into mind
As Olivia stirred
Time and times
And a half into destiny.

Then
The Unknown God
Called upon his heart
And Lock N. Load felt
The deep touch
Of forevermore.

It was
A vision of Grandpa Time
As a young lad
Clad in gold
From his skull cap
To his golden slippers
Adjusting
The celestial clocks
To coincide
With the spirit of the age
As Lock N. Load
And the children of promise
Approached nothingness.

It is
That nothingness
Is the domain
Of puppet masters
And they trigger
Outliving self
Across the minds
Of the living.

At the center
Of times and a half
Olivia from oblivion

Took the sword of Truth
To the throat of despair
As the puppet masters raced
Into another reality.

So
The puppet masters
Dug into a cloud
Of confusion
To alter their presence.

They became the language
Of sweet talking
Promising freedom
As they cut out
The heart of Truth.

Then
Grandpa Time took Lock N. Load
and the children of promise
Into a parabola of time
Where the celestial clocks
Spoke them
Into a two-dimensional reality.

Then
A portal opened
To The Spirit of Wisdom
And The Unknown God
Read them
Into always and forever.

So
Despair was the weapon
That the puppet masters used

To chain the hearts of the living
As the existential threat
Of dasein
Inflicted a destiny of angst
Upon the living.

Then
Olivia from oblivion
Circled Truth
With the body of becoming.

Then Lock N. Load set out
For the other side
Of the sky.

So
It was venturing
Into the unknown
As a portal opened
To the beyond.

There were
Trumpets arranged
In the moment
And Lock N. Load followed
The rhythm
Of the universe.

It was
The rise of pure music
In the blood
Of being toward Truth
That drove him

Into the deep touch
And Grandpa Time
Waved the dull round
Into a picture
Of always already there.

Then
Lock N. Load leaped
Into the other side
Of time and space
Until he reached
Into the domain
Of Truth.

Among the treasures there
The gift of faith
Granted the vision
Of what matters
As the close at hand
Triggered passage
Onto always and forever.

So
A house of many mansions
Shot through mind
And the heart matched
The chimes
Of the celestial clocks.

How
Eternity filled Lock N. Load
With the substance
Of being toward Truth
And The Word

Took him beside
Still waters.

Then
He slipped
Behind the mask
In the looking glass
Venturing
Into the substance
Of heart and mind.

Settling down in the garden
Of tables and chairs
Where angels
Gathered in time past
Lock N. Load launched
Into the unknown
Following the drift
Of pure music.

Near by
Overlooking a graveyard
A crow perched
On a tombstone
And the mystery of life
Filled being toward Truth
With awe.

It was
The sound of trumpets
Pyramiding through space
Until Grandpa Time
Harnessed what was there

And The Spirit of Wisdom
Circled
All and everything.

There was
A river of thought
That eased Lock N. Load
Into another reality
Where Truth dawned
Across time and space.

Then
The graves of time past
Stood on end
As Grandpa Time pulled
Hidden meaning
Into a vision of triumph
And a crow signaled
A new era.

Then
The garden of tables
And chairs burned
With Truth
And the sky opened
To The Unknown God.

Sharing space
The Unknown God
And Lock N. Load
Measured the expanse
With thought
As the children of promise
Carried life into forevermore.

Then
Olivia from oblivion
Appeared
In a looking glass
As the tombstones
Of being and nothingness
Traced hidden meaning
Into the heart
Of what matters.

To transcend
Time and space
To leap into the beyond
While anchored
In the here and now
Lock N. Load wove mind
Into The Spirit of Wisdom.

It was
The stretch
Of being toward Truth
Into possibility
That brought the unknown
Into view
As Olivia from oblivion
Took to the looking glass.

Then
Lock N. Load felt
The deep touch
As The Unknown God
Called upon his heart

While the puppet masters
Manipulated the here and now.

It is
The Truth
That time and times
And a half
Are being fulfilled
In the now.

So
The world spun
Into a new orbit
One of fear
And trepidation.

So
Olivia and the children
Of promise
Set out to focus
The breath of the living
As Lock N. Load
Bolted into the center
Of the puppet masters
His fight governed
By the power of The Word.

Then
The language of eternity
Rippled across the expanse
And Grandpa Time
Steadied his aim.

How
The blood of Truth

Brings life
To those fallen
Off the edge of faith.

So
The Spirit of Wisdom
Is the engine
Of The Unknown God.

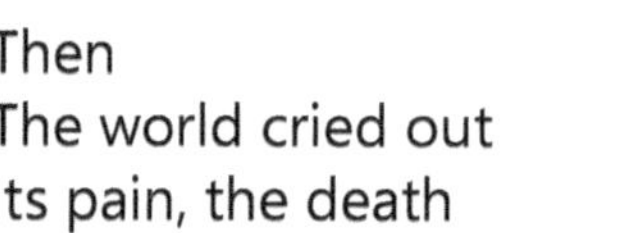

Then
The world cried out
Its pain, the death
Of populations
Rising into the heavens.

How
Cruel the puppet masters
That birthed
A pestilence of tens
Of thousands and the dead
Spoke into the minds
Of the puppet masters
Haunting them with the agony
Of the stricken.

So
What is justice
If they are not punished?

So
They hid the Truth
To the nations
Keeping them in the dark.

How
Different the outcome
Had the world known
About the plague
That the puppet masters
Conjured.

So
Lock N. Load launched
A task force
To guide him
In the governance
Of the plague
And Olivia from oblivion
Stood watch
Over a suffering world
Holding the hand
Of the afflicted
As the heroes of the times
Administered to their well-being.

Into battle
The heroes charged
Facing the disease head on
And the people banned together
Fighting for Truth
As the destiny of mankind.

So
The puppet masters
Were confronted
By a united world.

How
Their sinister plot

Was the signature
Of their own demise.

To roam
The frontier of mind
To fashion thought
To squeeze
Into the unknown
How
Being toward Truth thrives
While in pursuit
Of pure music.

It is
That the domain
Of possibility
Insights visions
That encompass
Being and nothingness
As the elements
Of phenomenal reality
A juxtaposition
Of hidden meaning
Triggering
The connectivity
Of things in themselves.

Then
Mind spins into an orbit
Of mystery
As the rhythm
Of pure music
Pronounces Truth

In the language
Of forevermore.

Then
The myths of time past
Awaken from the dead
And being toward Truth holds
Onto the life
Of the living moment
As times undress
The unknown.

So
There is a connection
Between what is there
And the beyond.

So
Truth speaks
To hidden meaning
As a portal
To the other side
Of the sky issues
An image
Of the everlasting.

There is
Substance to the time
When the deep touch
Reaches into mind
Offering the light
Through the one-dimensional
Reality
From The Unknown God.

The call of a crow
The call from the wilds
Brings heart close
To the movement of the earth
As being toward Truth
Fashions a will
After the dignity of creation.

There is
A triumphal entrance
Into phenomenal reality
Where things in themselves
Appear as the nobility
Of what matters
And the creatures
Of the earth celebrate
The living moment.

Then
To step away
From what is there
And pursue
Celestial dynasties
Where the stars
Bring light into darkness
How
Mind sees the divine purpose
Of being and nothingness
Through the inner eye.

It is
That the living moment
Issues the radiance
Of The Unknown God

And the presence
Of wonder and awe
As time releases
Hidden meaning
One day at a time.

So
There is veritable Truth
And that which is virtual
A seeming and deception
While veritable Truth
Points to The Word
As The Spirit of Wisdom
Drives substance
Into what matters.

Then
The crow pronounces life
Into the moment
And being toward Truth reads
The message
Of always and forever
Taking time and times
And a half
Into pure music
The speaking of veritable Truth.

In the center
Of what matters
Pure music feeds
The unknown
With treasures and images
As the heart

Of being toward Truth
Displaces time and space.

There is
The trumpet of victory
Cascading
Through the moment
When the mask
Of self-deception
Burns onto ash.

As the drums of eternity
Release a rhythm
To the bones of thought
That ache for Truth
The deep touch
Of The Unknown God
Creates fathoms
Of what matters.

There
In the passage of mind
Across horizons of thought
Being toward Truth finds
The mana of life
And the sky opens
To a chorus of the beyond.

How
The always already there
Defines the birth of hope
And The Word
Allows Truth to come
Into presence.

To see
Beyond the close at hand
And into the reaches
Of mind
The Spirit of Wisdom
Points to the way
The Truth and the life.

Then
The Word rubs life
Into a valley of dry bones.

Then
Time and space
Dissolve into a moment.

Then
Pure music parades
With an eternal wonder.

It was
That the puppet masters
Wanted to eliminate
Freedom
By controlling the thoughts
Of the people.

They wanted absolute power.

It was
The call upon the hearts
Of Lock N. Load, Olivia
And the children of promise

To preserve and protect
The freedom and rights
Of the people.

How
This conflict roared
Through the hollows
Of the dull round.

So
Grandpa Time
The figure of a faith
In The Unknown God
Fought against the efforts
Of the puppet masters.

The war of principalities
Raged on
As the celestial clocks
Clung to the rhythm
Of the universe
As Olivia from oblivion
Drew with a sword
Of Truth
And a dagger of life.

It was
The power
Of the puppet masters
Against the will
Of The Unknown God.

How
Eternity opened
The way of Truth and life

As Lock N. Load faced
The unknown.

It was
A war of minds
And a war of hearts
As time reached
Into possibility
And Lock N. Load traveled
Beyond time and space
As an attack
Upon this existential threat.

Then
The dull round fell
Before a rain of blood
And the battle ate
Life after life.

In the garden
Of tables and chairs
Mind sought
To uncover hidden meaning
As the sky looked on
Through a window to forevermore.

It was
That thoughts connected
To thought
Until the architecture
Of being and nothingness
Appeared in the expanse.

It was
A structure of elements
That emanated
Pure music
And time and space
Became the rhythm
Of heart
Through the center
Of what matters.

Dawning upon life
Mind eased
Into the light
Of always and forever
As the heat
Of the moment
Eclipsed dasein.

Suddenly
A portal opened
To the given
And mind placed
The image of Truth
Across the horizon.

Then
Heart followed
The drift of the unknown
Breathing in wonder
And being toward Truth
Climbed out of self
And into the radiance
Of the always already there.

From the close at hand
To the expanse
Treasures flourished
From The Unknown God
And heart warmed.

It was
Entrance into the deep touch
That brought
The vision of The Word
Into mind
And Truth unfolded
The mystery of life.

What was there
Defined the geometry
Of thought
And heart felt
The grace of the everlasting.

As the waters stilled
As the fog lifts away
The call of a crow
Speaks magic
Into the air
And time breathes in
The deep touch
Of The Spirit of Wisdom.

It is
The opening of a portal
To the other side
Of being and nothingness

That pulls a vision
Of peace
Beyond understanding
And The Word moves
Eternity into heart.

How
Being toward Truth at first light
Summons Truth into a reality
Far beyond the here and now
As the hidden meaning
Of time and times
And a half
Echoes across the waters
Of possibility.

Then
It all becomes
A two-dimensional image
Fixed in the moment
And mind follows traces to the origin
Of the sky.

It is
The end of nothingness
And the beginning
Of what matters
As life awakens
The bones of eternity
And heart tunes
Into the chimes
Of the celestial clocks.

Then
The grandeur

Of The Unknown God
Paints the living moment
With pure music
And mind passes
Into a looking glass
Of time and space.

There is
The call of the crow
To life
Onto the everlasting
That begets being toward Truth
Into the unknown
As hidden meaning
Lights the way to Truth.

So
The plague visited home
After home
And the dead and dying
Rotted in their beds.

It was
A time when laughter
Could not be found
And good humor
Wore rough edges.

Although
Lock N. Load fashioned hope
The nerves twitched and twisted
The face of a people
Longing for better times.

How
Thankful they were
To live another day
As the breaths of life
Became fewer and fewer.

Reluctant
To call it germ warfare
The world took a stand
And the puppet masters
Saw the falling of their plan.

It is
The spirit
Of The Unknown God
That brought hope
To the devastated
And it is
Looking into the eyes
Of death
That gathered the muscle
Of courage
As a people rose
Against the puppet masters.

So
These were hard times
As sores festered
In the lungs of the world
But heroes came
To bring good health
To the masses.

How
The puppet masters

Underestimated
The will of a people
And their faith in The Word.

What folly these puppet masters.

What darkness their hearts.

In the meadow
Of being and nothingness
Where time and space
Carry the heart
To celestial dynasties
Mind climbs out of self
And the image
Of being toward Truth kisses
The likeness of forevermore.

There
Growing into the moment
Trance takes the breath
Of what matters
And hidden meaning
Opens the way to possibility.

So
The unknown shares
Its mystery
With the voice of eternity
And mind speaks the language
Of pure music.

Then
The look of the deep touch
Covers being toward Truth
With the sky
Of the always already there.

How
The wind brings light
To the mystery of life
As heart drives the moment
When time and space
Fill life with life.

So
The end of hidden meaning
Brings the beginning
Of eternity
Where Truth rises
In the blood
And the dull round
Leaves a hollow
Of the existential moment.

Although
Time walks in circles
Purpose eclipses
Possibility
And the unknown sheds
Its mask of darkness.

There is
Only the deep touch
To pure music
Bringing the promise

Of forevermore
To the heart
As being toward Truth rests
With the peace
Beyond understanding.

Sitting in a stand
Of trees
Where the light
Filters through the leaves
And shadows cling
To time and space
Lock N. Load meditates
On The Word
As heart follows
The sounds of pure music.

As the looking glass
Of deep waters
Penetrates the moment
With passion
Lock N. Load empties
His mind
Until he feels
The awakening of what matters.

There is
The movement
Of earth sounds
Behind the mind
As Truth releases him
From the bondage
Of the puppet masters.

Then
Walking out
Of time and space
He gathers the drift
Of things in themselves.

There is beauty
In the forest
As the wilds speak
To his heart
And being toward Truth trumpets
Through the bones
Of hidden meaning.

Here
In this moment
Lock N. Load sees
Through his inner eye
And phenomenal reality
Connects to the beyond.

How
The always already there
Opens eternity
To the beat of his heat
And life dwells
In the living moment.

Then
The engine
Of The Unknown God
Drives Lock N. Load
Into the everlasting
As The Spirit of Wisdom

Issues the peace
Beyond understanding.

There is
Peace in his mind
And rest in his heart.

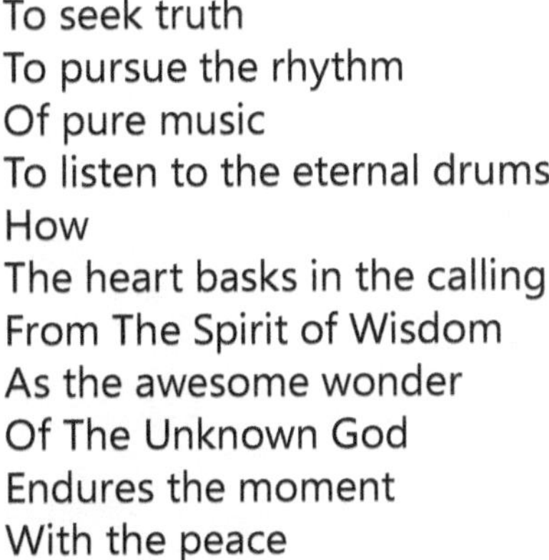

To seek truth
To pursue the rhythm
Of pure music
To listen to the eternal drums
How
The heart basks in the calling
From The Spirit of Wisdom
As the awesome wonder
Of The Unknown God
Endures the moment
With the peace
Beyond understanding.

It is
The power in the blood
Given in the fullness of time
That brings life
Onto forevermore
As being toward Truth opens
Self to The Word.

To accept the gift
From the always
Already there
Liberates the mind

From the concerns
Of the dull round
As the heart drinks in hope.

Then
The bells of eternity
Count the breaths
Of the everlasting
As time witnesses
The return of The Word.

There is
The heralding of the trumpet
That frees being toward Truth
Allowing the vision
Of life to awaken to Truth.

There is
A span of years
That promises a destiny
Of being
With The Unknown God
As the winds of forevermore
Fill the living with life.

So
There is a calling
To the heart
That takes the mind
Into the beyond
As the ache for Truth
Feeds upon The Word.

So
In our beginning there is life
Forevermore.

So
The puppet masters sent
A plague
Across the globe
And the world suffered
With a last breath
A cry for help.

For those who saw
The face of humanity
As figures of nothingness
Lock N. Load rose
The power of Truth
Against them
And pure music
Gave hope to the living.

How
The hour of infamy
Struck the world
As the puppet masters
Played their game.

Deep into meditation
Upon The Word
Lock N. Load felt the muscle
Of the Unknown God
And Olivia from oblivion
Showed him
The justice of Truth.

It was
Swift and it was true
As the puppet masters
Folded their lives with ashes.

Time and times
And a half passed
As the world struggled
Against the plague
And the survivors
Of this pestilence
Looked to The Word
For deliverance.

Then
Ten thousand, thousand
Angels encompassed the world
Showering the earth
With the strength
To endure.

Then
The puppet masters
Hid beneath mountains
As they trembled
Before their retribution.

Then
The Unknown God
Squeezed life
Out of them
And they fell
Into the lake of fire
For their second death.

SECTION 2

Around the Corner from Time and Space

Orchestrated by the hand
Of pure music
The artist composes
A vision of a castle
In the sky.

In the grip of the moment
Pure music catches the wind
From eternity
And trumpets salute
The way, the Truth and the life.

Although the artist meditates
In a wilderness of images
His thoughts convey
Hidden meaning
In time and space.

Among the fields
Of wonder he paints
The cry for Truth
Met by echoes
Of uncertainty.

Accepting himself
As believing toward Truth
He uncovers
The mystery of life

And the deception
Of being and time.

There is
The crawl of color
Across the sky
As the dawn of a new age
Brings trepidation.

In a looking glass
He sees
The language of a starry night
As time past leaves traces
To what matters.

Then
The rage in the night
Witnesses
The movement into ashes
As a fallen star
Strikes the earth
With muscle and blood.

The artist
Testifies to the course
Of the children of promise
Under the steel fist
Of persecution.

So
It was the death
Of Truth
That he painted

From the darkness
In a cruel dungeon.

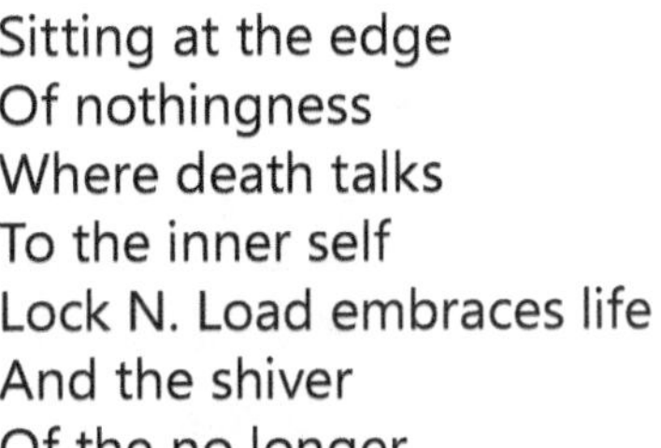

Sitting at the edge
Of nothingness
Where death talks
To the inner self
Lock N. Load embraces life
And the shiver
Of the no longer
Surrounds the sky.

It is
A trembling of mind
That centers will
Upon the moment
When possibility surges
Into the mainstream
Of time and space
As the dull round
Waits for the beginning
Of forevermore.

How
Eternity calls his name
From the wilds
Of what is there
And the inner eye
Moves curiosity
Through time.

Then
Lock N. Load leaps
Into a portal
To the beyond
As pure music fills
Time and space
With the deep touch
And he believes himself
Toward The Word.

So
Being toward Truth is
Being toward
The Unknown God
As a prayer eclipses
Nothingness
And Olivia from oblivion
Holds the treasures
Of Truth in his heart.

She takes to the moment
When the always already there
Reveals things in themselves
And Lock N. Load
Pours his substance
Into the light
Of the everlasting.

Then
Olivia releases
Hidden meaning
And an epiphany
Of being and nothingness
Throbs the heart
As Truth moves

With the language
Of silence.

As the age
Of the puppet masters
Rises into darkness
And the death of freedom
Falls between the cracks
Lock N. Load reads
The deep touch
Of The Spirit of Wisdom
In the language of hope.

Olivia from oblivion
Flexes the muscle
Of the tribe
And the war of principalities
Turns into a blood bath
With the dead feasting on life.

It is
That the trumpet
Of freedom summons
Truth into the moment
As the wilds focus
Upon the authentic article.

It is
That the puppet masters
Wear the mask
Of self-deception
As they squander life
And the tribe advances

Wearing the armor
Of pure music.

Then
The puppet masters
Turn to ash
Consumed away
By their hunger for power
And Lock N. Load meditates
On The Word
Where the life of Truth
Flourishes.

There is
In the looking glass of mind
The struggle
Of being and nothingness
As trance carries
Lock N. Load into the beyond.

There
Pure music sings
The authentic article
Into time and space
As the tribe
Triumphs over tyranny.

So
There is no hope
For the puppet masters
And the second death
Is their destiny.

When time and times
And a half reveal
The mystery of life
And heart feels the deep touch
Of what matters
Being toward Truth rises
With the integrity
Of the authentic article
As The Spirit of Wisdom
Endows mind with Truth.

So
The moment of this epiphany
Deconstructs the dull round
And forevermore liberates self.

Then
Pure music eclipses self-deception.

Then
Time and space fold
Into a two-dimensional reality
And things in themselves
Dance on the tongue
Of being and nothingness.

It is
To perceive the movement
When the inner eye
Registers hidden meaning
And mind fathoms
The song of silence
That Truth appears
Between the lines
Of what is there

In a language
Of celestial clocks.

To grasp
The unknown requires
A faith
Through The Spirit of Wisdom
As being toward Truth
Moves into possibility
And the shadows of eternity
Follow mind
Through the liberation of self.

How
Freedom talks
To the heart
Of being toward Truth
Undressing the drift
Of the deep touch.

Then
Belief makes possibility
Into the evidence
Of the always already there.

So
The Unknown God is
Of the always already there
Only.

Bonded by the power
Streaming from the pursuit
Of Truth

Lock N. Load and Olivia
From oblivion grew
Into a love with pure music
As their legacy.

As they shared the deep touch
They built a union
Based on faith
In The Unknown God
And they worshiped The Word
Throughout the living moment.

How
Angels applauded them
As time and space
Became the language
Of forevermore
As Olivia danced
On a horizon
Of beauty and wonder
And Lock N. Load carved
Her name in his heart.

Entwined together
They filled time
With the essence of life
As things in themselves
Revealed hidden meaning.

When Lock N. Load entered trance
Images of the beyond spoke
Through an existential threat
But the mystery
Of The Spirit of Wisdom
Lighted the way to Truth.

Then
The passion of pure music
Carried them into a reality
Of always and forever
As they eclipsed
Self-deception
And the mask of bad faith
Withered away.

They were naked
Before The Unknown God
Stripped of embellishment
When they beheld
The treasure of their bond.

How
True love endures all things
And is a blessing
From The Unknown God.

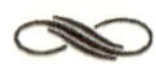

While in trance
Time and space dissolve
Into The Spirit of Wisdom
And being toward Truth approaches
The Unknown God.

Visions swirl
Into images of pure music
As trance takes to the deep touch.

Then
Mind leaps
Into the unknown

As possibility basks
In the light of The Word.

In the interstices
Of the close at hand
A looking glass reveals
Hidden meaning
While the beyond fills heart
With the passion
Of the always already there.

How
The moment brings
The authentic article
Across the life
Of being toward Truth
And the dull round
Speaks eternity
Into the heart
An epiphany of forevermore.

Then
The inner eye sees
The war of principalities
As being and nothingness
Shatter the here and now.

So
The moment wrestles
With the pains of the dying
And the language
Of the given weeps
Over the graves
Of the no longer.

How
A fire burns in the heart
Reaching for Truth
As pure music encompasses
Horizons of thought.

Then
Being toward Truth leaves
The shadows of despair
Following the light
Of The Word
And time and space
Feed life
Through meditation.

So
The plague swept
Across the globe
And nation after nation
Crippled by the virus
Fell into depression.

In the streets
Bodies piled as victims
And the puppet masters
Laughed at their demise
Because it meant
That they would rule
The world.

So
They saw this plague
As an opportunity

To gain power
Over all the people.

Then
Lock N. Load, Olivia
From oblivion and the tribe
Brewed an antidote
And nation after nation
Returned to full strength.

How
The puppet masters
Retreated in their shame.

As time passed
The nations stoned
The puppet masters
And they fell into ashes
Leaving no trace
Except a bitter memory.

So
The world turned to Truth
And they breathed
The strength
Of The Unknown God.

It was
The end of terror
And the end of the plague.

There was
Singing in the streets
Hymn after hymn
That praised The Worde

And the bells of freedom
Offered tribute
To the glory
Of The Unknown God.

So
The best laid plans
Of mice and men
Could not match
The way
The Truth and the life.

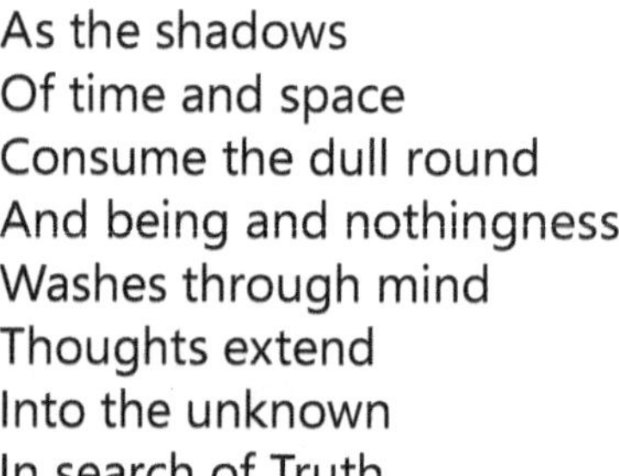

As the shadows
Of time and space
Consume the dull round
And being and nothingness
Washes through mind
Thoughts extend
Into the unknown
In search of Truth.

Because being toward Truth
As the presence of the spirit
Navigates
Through possibility
Onto things in themselves
That the moment
Triggers the inner eye
Into reading the language
Of pure music.

Although
The melody of the wilds

Establishes freedom
In the heart
And the world looks
To the celestial clocks
For guidance
The Unknown God
Moves life
Into what matters.

How
Eternity begins in the now
With images
From the close at hand
And being toward Truth
Toward The Word
Liberates mind.

Then
The trance carries
The realities
Of time and space
Into the frontier
Of mind
As the spirit grasps life.

There is
Quiet among the wilds
As the steady pace of passion
Drives meaning into the moment
And the sun warms
The earth of being toward Truth.

It is
That time future
Passes through time present

Onto time past
As the shadows
Of what is there
Walk through the looking glass
Of forevermore.

It was
In the deep reaches
Of time and space
That trance took
Being and nothingness
Into the blood
Of being toward Truth.

Then
The heart soared
Into the unknown
Grasping the magnitude
Of hidden meaning
As the anthem of Truth
Emptied tears of want
Into the barriers of possibility.

Although
The pain of nothingness
Crippled mind
There was aa light
From the beyond
That spoke
The language of hope.

To endure the deception
Of the puppet masters

How
The hunger for power
Throws mud
In the face
Of The Unknown God
As the faithful prepare
For battle.

How truth speaks
Through darkness
Bringing light
To the multitudes
And the puppet masters
Sleep in their ashes.

There is
No hope for the godless.

As time and space
Yield to the power
Of Truth
Mind leaps into the always
Already there
As the deep touch carries thought
With a free spirit.

Then
Being toward Truth
Toward The Unknown God
Triumphs
Over the oppressors
And liberty chimes
The bells of eternity.

So
The one man band
With the gold dust twins
Wooed a nation
And the world wept
With awe.

It was
In a concert at the edge
Of time and space
That the dull round
Slipped into the4 sea
And a people washed away
With Truth.

So
The songs carried
The moment
Into a river of dreams
As pure music danced
With the freedom
Of living blood.

Then
A generation stood
Among the stars
As the moon covered them
With the light of eternity
And they followed
Their dreams
Into the everlasting.

It was
That a one man band
Brought The Spirit of Wisdom

Into the heat
Of being and nothingness
And being toward Truth
Fought tyranny
Through the inner eye.

Then
A house of many mansions
Rose into the sky
As life lived
Toward The Unknown God
Allowing forevermore
To step into the heart
Of what matters.

So
Eternity rubbed life
Into being toward Truth.

So
The dull round heeded
The whispers in the wind.

So
The moment eclipsed time and space.

Revealed to the moment
When pure music shown
Through the looking glass
Of the close at hand
Mind stepped
Into the other side
Of phenomenal reality.

There was
Truth cascading
Through time and space
As The Spirit of Wisdom
Spoke the language
Of being and nothingness.

There was
The breath of freedom
Filling life
With awe and wonder
As thoughts followed
The trace
To the authentic article.

There was
The presence
Of The Unknown God
In the workings
Of time and space
As the engine of Truth
Overpowered
Self-deception.

Then
Being toward Truth leaped
Into horizons of reality
As the shadows
Cried out for mercy.

Although
The war of principalities
Expanded darkness
Trance took the moment

Into the broken bones
Of life.

For a while
Heart bled in open places
As trumpets heralded
The other side of the sky.

Then
Mind traveled
Into the unknown
As thoughts unearthed
The substance
Of the here and now.

Anchored in Truth
Being toward Truth surfaced
And the spirit as nonbeing
Entered the domain
Of forevermore.

Freedom grows
In as heart of pure music
As time drops the chains
Of self-deception
And visions circulate
Through the inner eye.

Off in a horizon
Of thoughts
Traces to true love
Dance to the silence
Of the moment.

There are
Countless echoes
In the heart
As shadows cover
The world
And memories of her face
Occupy the inescapable
Here and now.

How
The treasures of her kisses
Rise above what matters
And in the hollows
Of time she hides
Secrets of eternity.

She is lady liberty
And the breath
Of forevermore
Caresses the moment
With the deep touch.

The invincibility of her eyes
Conquers the trembling
Of bones
As she passes through mind.

How
True loves cleanses time
With the blood of eternity
As life eases
Into being toward Truth.

There is
An anthem in the wind

Conquering Corrupter
In its deceit
As freedom speaks
Truth to the heart
And mountains color
The embrace of the always
Already there.

There is
Truth to the moment
That lady liberty prepares
As she turns the wilds
Into a garden
Of tables and chairs.

Her splendor
A privilege to serve.

As the puppet masters
Strangled life from the living
The heart of freedom,
Pounded times and a half
Into the moment
And the war of principalities
Raged on.

It was
Lady liberty
That held a fortress
Of Truth
And Olivia from oblivion
Equipped herself
With arms for battle.

So
There was deception
In the wind
And a world
Forgot discernment
Crying out
For deliverance.

It was
Mind control
That the puppet masters
Thought would prove
Victorious
But Lock N. Load
Had not given
Into their deceit.

So
The tribe was
A bastion of Truth
Founded upon The Word
And the tribe drew
Upon the power
Of The Unknown God
For strength.

Then
Pure music poured
Upon the world
And the faithful stood tall
Before the face of tyranny.

While the puppet masters
Tried to smother Truth
The tribe looked

To The Word
Finding freedom
In the way
The Truth and the life.

What folly
In the heart
Of the puppet masters
Thinking they could rule
Over the faithful
That held onto the freedom
Of a pure heart and clear mind.

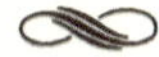

It was
The mechanics of mind
That wrote the language
Of being and nothingness
An apparatus
Deciphering time and space
And searching for Truth.

It was
The hidden meaning
In the close at hand
That held possibility
And it was
Thought that pried open
The unknown
Revealing things in themselves.

The failure
To read between the lines
Leads to the darkness

Of self-deception
As the puppet masters
Reveal their corrupt hearts.

How
Ugly the corrupt hearts.

Then
Olivia from oblivion struck
The oppressors
With the sword of Truth
And the puppet masters
Cried out for mercy.

It is
That lady liberty
Guided by The Word
Fashioned justice
As the tribe forms
An immutable force
And the world looks
To the power
Of The Unknown God
To fight the good fight.

It is
Truth that conquers
Oppression
Freeing hearts and minds
From the grip
Of deception
As the tribe vanquishes
Evil intent.

Then
Lock N. Load
Leaves his meditation
To lance Corrupter
And time and times
And a half roll
Into the fullness of time.

Freedom speaks the language of Truth.

Off in the distance
A crow calls
And the wilds breathe
The freedom
Of being toward Truth
As the day issues
The birth of a moment.

It is
In the presence of the now
That the face of Truth
Bears the image of forevermore
And time slips into memories
Of the deep touch.

How
A vision of the always
Already there opens possibility
Allowing faith
To deliver the spirit
Of the source of it all
To The Unknown God.

Then
The crow brings
The bead of life
As the deep touch
Of always and forever
Shines light into mind.

How
The heart bathes
In the blood of Truth
And grows strong
Among the hymns
Of The Word.

So
It was Olivia
From oblivion who taught
Life through her dance
Upon the horizons
As phenomenal reality
Erased being and nothingness.

Then
A void covered timer
As an ach punctured muscle
And space evacuated the moment
As trance took to the crow.

Within
The reaches of time and space
A looking glass
Allows the vision
Of forevermore to appear
And Olivia from oblivion

Rises into the given
With an epiphany in her heart.

Then
The crow speaks Truth
Into being toward Truth.

There is
A bird in his ear
With the song of spring
As the sun warms his bones
And eternity fills
His heart with visions
Of pure music.

How
The world trembles
Through the here and now
As he leaps beyond the sky
And the trumpets
Of The Spirit of Wisdom
Carry him through the unknown.

Awakening to the moment
He looks through the gravity
Of time and space
Searching for the rebirth of love
As the blossoms
Of spring perfume the air.

There is
The promise of the second birth
Carried by angels

To his heart
As the sun embraces him
With visions of possibility.

So
It is tomorrow that seeds dreams
Of forevermore
As he listens to the anthem
Of the free and brave
As the earth
Longs for lady liberty.

Then
The wilds emanate
A new beginning
With the deep touch
Of The Word as he feels life
Return to his being toward Truth.

How
Precious the moment
When he beholds the glory
Of The Unknown God
As the day rises
With the always already there.

So
The song of spring issues
Life onto forevermore.

In the garden
Of tables and chairs
The tribe gathers

To listen to the wisdom
Of The Spirit of Wisdom.

It is
The pure music of faith
That bonds with flesh and blood
As mind drinks in
And under being toward Truth
As the awesome beauty
Of the wilds liberates
The cry for freedom.

Then
The tribe takes to the wind
Armed with Truth
As each brings life to battle.

So
Each faces the puppet masters
With the power
Of The Unknown God
And ten thousand thousand angels
Eclipse the godless
As the free spirits
Of the tribe don
The form of warriors
For the faith.

There is
No adversary that can
Overpower the Truth
As the tribe rises
To the demise
Of mind control.

So
The tribe left
The garden of tables and chairs
To battle the principalities of darkness.

When being toward Truth
Enters nothingness
The odor of the void
Fills the lungs with despair
And the taste of death
Heaves the gut.

There is
The cold touch of the no longer
In the bones
As the dirge of infamy
Drowns the spirit.

As mind battles
For clarity
And the heart
Longs for purity
Being toward Truth feels
The existential moment
And tears fall from the sky.

How
Nightmares wrestle
Through times and a half
And the blood
Of being toward Truth dries
Into mounds of ash.

It is
Through being in nothingness
That the spirit learns
Of separation
From The Unknown God
But a seed is planted
A seed of hope.

Then
The living moment returns
And nothingness drops away.

There is
A house of many mansions
At the horizon
As the sun rises
In the heart
And being toward Truth sees
The given
As a beauteous wonder.

To be
A child of The Unknown God
How love dwells in the promise
Of eternal life.

An old friend
Of years and years
The crow tells the heart
That times have passed
As the aches of being old
Grow memories, but giving up
Is out of the question.

It is
To battle back to life
When it seems
That time has run out
That being toward Truth looks
Through the eyes of destiny
And there are still
Songs to sing.

Although thee passage of time
Cripples the body
Mind leaps into life
And images of what matters
Stir the heart
With thankfulness.

Then
A vision returns living
To the moment
And the inner eye
Looks for a portal
To Truth.

Then
The power of The Unknown God
Takes being toward Truth
Through a looking glass
As the image
Of forevermore dances
Across horizons of time.

To place self
Into the living moment
How
The energy in The Spirit of Wisdom

Restores the spirit
As the ache of ages
Fortifies the muscle
Of being toward Truth
And the crow
That old friend, shares
The secrets of the unknown.

So
The moment is vivid
When the deep touch
Reaches into mind
And thoughts awaken
To the here and now.

There are songs to sing
And drums to pound
As the rhythm
Of pure music
Places treasures
With the bread of life.

So
It was that a plague
Was administered
By the puppet masters
A cruel affliction
That murdered a multitude
Across the globe.

The reasoning
Of the puppet masters
Was simple

But no less sinister:
To gain control of the world
Through inflicting
A dreaded disease.

To inflict fear
Across the dull round
They believed
Would bring the world
To its knees
But they underestimated
The spirit of the tribe.

The stars and stripes forever
Faced the virus head on
With the vigor known
To free spirits
As they probed
The hidden meaning
Locked inside the plague.

It was
Lady liberty that arrested
The affliction
Taking away its sinister will.

It was
A tribe grounded in Truth
A nation of one people
Free spirits founded
Upon the belief
That all mankind
Was composed
Of equal individuals
And they knew the way

To Truth and life.
What
Folly in the hearts
Of the puppet masters
As they crowned
In their own blood.

So
The nations cried out
For retribution
Looking to Corrupter
For a pound of flesh.

As being toward Truth feels
The muscle of The Spirit of Wisdom
The substance of what matters
Charges mind with visions
Of pure music
And time and space
Ready the wings into the unknown.

To believe
In The Unknown God
As presence
In infinite possibility
How
The moment takes Truth
As the given
And heart dwells
With the deep touch.

Then
Horizons open

To the looking glass
Of the minute particular
As thoughts traverse
Being and nothingness
Into a vertical column of time
Where hidden meaning
Reveals the way
The Truth and the life.

It is
In the close at hand
That a portal
Takes mind
Into the always
Already there
And an epiphany
Releases the spirit
Into the liberty
Of being toward Truth.

Then

The earth of pure music
Allows the vision to the beyond
And the mystery of life
Fills mind
With what matters.

So
The here and now
Reclaims Truth from possibility
As The Word presents
The moment
Of eternal freedom
Where self endures
Onto forevermore.

So
This life allows passage
Into the awe and wonder
Of being in the presence
With The Unknown God.

So
Being toward Truth lives
In Truth through the deep touch.

So
It is that a pure heart
Comes through the deep touch
Of The Unknown God
As The Word works through faith.

It is
A gift to the believer
A miracle
From the reality of Truth.

In the darkness of depravity
There is no hope
To see the light of eternity
Through the inner eye.

It is
Being through the looking glass
That allows Truth
To reckon pure music
As the mystery of life
Reflects the way
The Truth and the life.

How
A vision of what matters
Opens the heart
To the everlasting
As the mind clears.

So
The trials and temptations
Of the world fall away
As being toward Truth emerges
Into the wonder of the always
Already there and the sense
Of The Spirit of Wisdom speaks
The language of deliverance.

All the while The Word
Unites the spirit
To the freedom of forevermore
As the heart holds the treasures
Of immaculate grace.

Then
Time and space yield
To Truth
As pure music guides
Times and a half
Through the eye of a needle.

There is
Possibility of Truth
That governs all and everything
And the possibility
Of The Unknown God
Who is of time past
Time present and time future

All at once
In a vertical column of time.

The rule
Of the puppet masters
In the age of affliction
As the world burns
With conflict
And freedom sings a song
Of pure music
Into the lives of the living.

How
The wings of eternity take
Times and a half
Into the light of liberty
As the window
To forevermore looks
Onto being and nothingness
And the struggle for the peace
Beyond understanding
Envelops the moment.

Then
The tongues
Of the puppet masters
Turn to ash
As their message
Defies reason.

How
their iron hand
holds a heart of stone.

There is
A promise in the wind
That secures freedom
Across the lands
And a harvest of souls
Trumpets victory
Over the oppressors.

To be
In the presence
Of a driving force
That brings liberty
How
The will of being toward Truth
Overcomes tyranny
As the stars and stripes
Sings an anthem
Of pure music
Into the heart
Of a hungry world.

Then
The puppet masters crumble
In the bones of its desire
To rule the world.

So
Truth liberates a world
That lived in the chains
Of deceit
And words of deception.

∞

It is
Lock N. Load and Olivia
From oblivion
Who step into another reality
In search for Truth.

It is
Through a looking glass
That they go
Following the rhythm
Of pure music into the expanse
As the unknown stretches
Thought across a parabola of time.

Then
Appearing in the flesh of Truth
The Word stands
At the gate to eternity
As the wind of kingdom come
Liberates being toward Truth
From the chains of the dull round.

Through meditation
They traverse time and space
To the other side of the sky
As the breath of the everlasting
Fills them with awe and wonder
As they spirit Truth
Into being toward Truth.

There is
A song raised in their hearts
As melody driven by the unknown
An anthem of freedom
An epiphany

From the always already there
And they leap out of themselves
Into The Spirit of Wisdom
The vast regions of peace
The temple of Truth
The splendor of what matters.

Then
Time and space of the minute particular
As evidence in the close at hand
Anchors their hearts
As their minds find
The clarity of the given
And Truth embraces their spirit.

Then
The mystery of life
Takes them into the beyond
And they hear the language
Of a vertical column of time.

How
Memories that they share
Shower them with the way
The Truth and the life
As The Unknown God
Pronounces their names
In eternity.

∞

SECTION 3

The beginning of the sky

Entering nonbeing
Where the inner eye senses a way
Through being and nothingness
Being toward Truth unravels
The mystery of life
As trance takes
To a looking glass.

Then
Images of Truth
Dance at the horizon
Of time and space
While self feeds
Upon The Spirit of Wisdom.

There is
An opening to a reality
Beyond thought
Where pure music defines
Time present
As the gathering
Of Truth through hope
And the bells of eternity
Awaken the moment
To the deep touch.

As nonbeing
The self travels through the unknown

As the spirit
Of a clear mind and pure heart.

It is
Through The Unknown God
That a three-dimensional reality
Is formed
As the foundation
Of all and everything
While mind trances
Through a multitude of realities.

So
The here and now anchors
Being toward Truth
In phenomenal reality
As mind traverses
Infinite possibility
Where nonbeing experiences
The breath of life.

How
Time future speaks
To time past
Through time present
As being toward Truth
Launches into the mystery of life
The realities of being
And nothingness.

So
Nonbeing walks around the moons
Of possibility

As the cosmic clock encompasses
All of time and space.

To probe the unknown
And gather the secrets
Of being and nothingness
Being toward Truth enters trance
And the mysteries of life
Paint an image of pure music
Read by the inner eye.

There is
A mountain of Truth
That staggers mind
As thoughts climb
Into the other side
Of the sky
And an epiphany
Through time and space
Translates the doctrine
Of the landscape.

Then
The rhythm of celestial clocks
Pronounces the life
Of the living moment
As phenomenal reality
Signals the deep touch
To stir times and a half.

So
Time present unearths
The connection

Between the here and now
And the beyond
As the moment traces
The palm at the end of mind.

To read
The signature of life
Being toward Truth lifts
The mask of self-deception
Discarding it with the death
Of time and space.

How
The geometry
Of what is there
Configures the unknown
Into pure music
And thought sees eternity
In a grain of sand.

Then
The echoes of time past
Trigger a vision
Of The Spirit of Wisdom
Through the deep touch.

So
The sky cracks open
And the blood of possibility
Flows with the unknown
Into the heart of being toward Truth.

∞

Within the fortress of faith
Being toward Truth reflects
Upon The Word
As time present leaves
The dull round.

There is the glory of The Unknown God
Shining on the spirit
Of a life that transcends
Being and time
As mind witnesses
The way
The Truth and the life.

Then
The moment opens
To visions of possibility
As the existence of Truth
Moves the heart
Into the deep touch.

How
Radiant the passage
To forevermore
As blessed assurance
Guides the mind
And guards the heart.

So
Eternity is in
The breath of pure music
Delivering being toward Truth
To what matters most.

Although
The language of being
An nothingness
Carves a hollow in the heart
Faith fills the moment
With the peace beyond
Understanding.

So
There is a garden of beauty
In the mind
As the inner eye bathes
In the splendor
Of The Unknown God.

It is
Through time and space
That being toward Truth
Tales a leap of faith
As the call to worship
Unveils the mystery of life.

Then
The image of Truth carries
The bones of what is there
Into the smile
Of the everlasting.

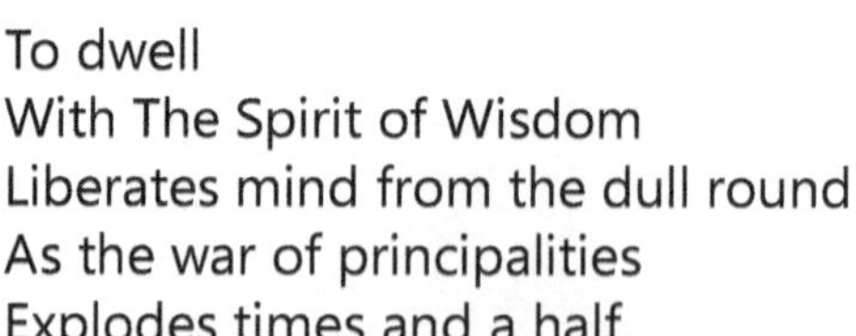

To dwell
With The Spirit of Wisdom
Liberates mind from the dull round
As the war of principalities
Explodes times and a half.

Pulling together
The spirit and the domain
Of the here and now
Allows the advance
Into the unknown
Where possibility
Where all and everything
Carries thought
Beyond phenomenal reality
In waves of pure music.

Once there
The heart stirs with the language
Of the everlasting
And the mystery of life reveals
Blessed assurance
Through the inner eye.

How
Being toward Truth feels
The authentic article
Through things in themselves
As the here and now
Speak Truth
Through the presence
Of The Unknown God
As thee sense
Of what matters eclipses
Being and nothingness.

So
Mind enters a portal
To a vertical column of time
Where Truth stands tall and solid
As an epiphany of The Word allows

The dance of freedom
Into forevermore.

Then
The heart feels
The pulse of The Spirit of Wisdom
As horizons of what matters
Reveal the authentic article
Through the liberation
Of the world.

Then
The moment takes
The breath of being toward Truth
Into visions of the deep touch
And the always already there
spirits time onto the edge
Of the here and now.

So
The puppet masters spread
Their deception across the land
And their deceit
Rotted the brains of the populace
With confusion.

It was
That darkness encompassed
The world with doublespeak
And Truth lost its way.

Then
Lock N. Load took to the wind

As his pure heart and clear mind
Separated times and a half
With pure music.

There was
A hunger for power re
In the puppet masters
That shook the ground
Of a world facing death
But Lock N. Load
Took the lead to the light
Of The Unknown God
As his tribe fought
The principalities of evil.

Then
The free spirits rose
From the rubble
With the knowledge and faith
In The Word
As trumpets of liberty
Cast away the chains
Of ignorance.

Although
The puppet masters sought
To control all minds
Lock N. Load and Olivia
Took the tribe into battle
For Truth and justice.

Although
The twisted words
Of the puppet masters
Crippled some

The Spirit of Wisdom
Brought light
Into an age of darkness.

Although
The earth trembled
Beneath the weight
Of the puppet masters
Truth rang clearly
In the hearts and minds
Of free spirits.

With the indwelling
Of The Word
Being toward Truth searches
The domain of Truth
As time and space
Reveal the launching
Of trance into the unknown.

It is
In the now
That what matters leaps
Through a looking glass
Reaching the other side
Of being and nothingness.

Then
A river of thought
Carries whispers
Into the beyond
As mind reaches

Into possibility
Through the deep touch.

On the wings
Of forevermore
With an anchor
In the close at hand
Being toward Truth follows
The Spirit of Wisdom
Into an epiphany
Of pure music.

Then
All phenomenal reality
Dances upon the tongue
Of possibility
As passion rives
A song into the heart
Of the living moment
And the dull round listens
To the call
Of the always already there.

To understand
The reaches of time and space
And to grasp the wits
Of forevermore
How thoughts proceed
With the vision of a clear mind
Into the wilds of the unknown.

So
Trumpets of the age
Pronounce the destiny
Of being and nothingness

The war of principalities
As victory goes to the faithful
Those who took
A leap of faith into the love
Of The Unknown God.

Following the echoes
Of pure music
Reaching the deep touch
Of The Spirit of Wisdom
The inner eye liberates mind
From the darkness
Of the dull round
As being toward Truth
Traverses the expanse
Of the unknown
And heart pounds
The freedom of forevermore.

It is
That time and space
Of another reality
Occupy the moment
And trumpets speak
The language
Of hidden meaning.

Then
Thoughts reflect
In a looking glass
Where Truth rises
In the light
Of the everlasting

As echoes of time past
Pronounce the freedom
Of being toward Truth.

Then
The need for peace
Beyond understanding
Finds the embrace
Of The Word
As the unknown pictures
The way
The Truth and the life.

So
In time present
The rhythm of pure music
Takes the spirit
Of things in themselves
Into the muscle of mind
And thoughts drive
The moment
Into the always already there.

How
The earth of being and nothingness
Unwinds the unknown
Revealing the mystery of life
As pure music
And Truth lights the hollows
Of hidden meaning.

As time future
Dances upon horizons
Of possibility
The Unknown God

Allows being toward Truth
To be.

When life is at the door
And a percussion of thoughts
Pounds the rhythm
Of pure music
Being toward Truth dances
In shades of blue
And mind eats the moment.

As the mask
Of self-deception falls
Into the pit of the no longer
The inner eye sees clearly
In the looking glass
A vision of what matters.

Then
The war of principalities
Crashes time present
And the earth moves
Into another reality.

There is
The anthem of Truth
Bringing hope
To the dull round
As the light of eternity
Rises in the heart.

So
In a universe

Of endless possibility
Nothing is impossible:
Hence, the existence of God.

Then
The moment absorbs
Time and space
As being toward Truth listens
To the call of the wilds.

Along the way
Into the mystery of life
Mind engages
The anatomy of being
And nothingness
Gathering the milestones
To eternity.

So
The heart of times and a half
Feels the splendor
Of The Unknown God
As the deep touch signals
The way, the Truth, and the life.

How
The breath of life
Deciphers hidden meaning
As the shadows
On the cave wall speak
Truth to being toward Truth.

Then
The cup overflows.

∞

The bones of eternity
Awaken to the trumpets
Of pure music
As the here and now
Drinks in the deep touch.

Then
Being toward Truth soars
Upon the wings
Of The Spirit of Wisdom
And the blue of what matters
Opens the sky to forevermore.

How
Savage the twists
Of language
That dismembers Truth
As the dull round
Falls apart
And the grave of reason
Buries hope
In the forgotten.

In the wind
Is the odor of the dead
And life is forgotten.

Then
Being and nothingness
Fills the moment
With brash strokes
Of hidden meaning.

To gather
The lost thoughts

Of understanding
The deep touch liberates
Mind from the cage
Of time present
As the other side of what is there
Offers the authentic article
To the living of life.

The wicked toss and turn
The language into a noose
That hangs understanding
And with a dagger slashes
The throat of reason.

How
Precious is freedom
Fed by Truth
The anthem marching
With the blood
Of pure music.

Stand strong in the storm
Of the puppet masters.

It is
In the wilderness
Of times and a half
That Truth speaks
With a radiant voice
As being and nothingness
Define the existential moment.

Arising in mind
The dawn of a new sun
Brings the light of wonder
As thoughts trace hidden meaning
Through a looking glass.

Then
The language of the deep touch
Arranges pure music in the heart
As the mystery of life
Dances upon horizons
Of time and space.

Understanding the way
The Truth and the life
Brings echoes of a song
An anthem of liberty
As The Spirit of Wisdom
Nourishes being toward Truth
As what matters
Becomes the breath
Of the authentic article.

Following the milestones
Of freedom
Through the geometry
Of times and a half
Emanates the call toward Truth
And mind reaches
Into things in themselves.

Then
The natural elements
Of being and nothingness
Reveal the face of possibility

Behind the mask
Of self-deception
As being toward Truth
Eases into meditation.

Although
The steppingstones of liberty
Follow traces into the unknown
The here and now
Breeds life into the moment
And the purpose
Of the wilderness
Carries that life
With blessed assurance.

So
Truth lives in the dawn of faith.

On the front lines
Of the war of principalities
The tribe digs in under fire
And death seems closer
Than life.

It is
That rifle fire
Defines the moment
As blood soaks the earth
And time present
Lies in an open grave.

To be
Beyond thought

Mind suspends all
And everything
As survival governs
Time and space
And the heart races
With anticipation.

Then
Silence walks
Across the battlefield
And wounds from the encounter
Speak their pain.

How
Being toward Truth holds fast
To reprieve
And the tribe gathers
Casualties.

So
Soldiers of Truth and justice
Carry life to the edge
Of the existential moment
As the expanse penetrates
That moment with tolling bells
And shadows no longer move.

Then
The wind quiets the battlefield
As the smell of death
Ripens time and space
And the tribe collects
The bones of the lost.

When the war
Of principalities ends

And the tribe proves victorious
Freedom stands tall
And marches to the homeland.

So
The heart of the tribe spirits liberty.

So
The mind of the tribe
Finds peace in preparedness.

So
The language of the wilds
Speaks Truth
Through a looing glass
Where images replace shadows
And mind turns to faith.

To understand
Things in themselves
To gras
The calculus of the living moment
How
Feeble the workings of dasein
As being toward Truth reaches
Through the unknown
To The Spirit of Wisdom
Producing and archeology
Of thought.

Then
The deep touch unearths
The rhythm of pure music

And the here and now
Allows the vision
Of the everlasting.

So
It is a matter
Of being toward death
That undresses the folly
Of self-deception
As dasein wears
The mask of uncertainty.

To the faithless
The self is a pawn
Of possibility
Without the will to be
But with the hunger
For self-aggrandizement
And Truth becomes a fiction
Of the weak minded.

So
All is relative in shades of gray.

So
Life is the beginning of death.

So
The purpose of dasein
Is to seek power.

How
Hollow the presence
Of the faithless
That thinks itself capable
Of discernment.

So
Darkness is the center
Of the existential moment.

As mind throttles
Into things in themselves
And time shifts into a moment
With The Spirit of Wisdom
The heart of being toward Truth
Feels the always already there.

Then
Mind follows the language
Of being and nothingness
Until the inner eye
Unearths hidden meaning.

It is
Pure music that wills
The deep touch
To liberate the here and now
From the constraints
Of the dull round
Of linear time and space
As the breath
Of a vertical column of time
Fills the moment with epiphany.

When
The shadows of self-deception
Sink into the abyss
Being toward Truth climbs
Out of self

And the now pours
The authentic article
Into heart.

Pyramiding through what is there
Mind travels
Into the always already there
Where being and nothingness
Steps into silence.

Then
The look of the beyond
Calls upon the light
Of the everlasting
And freedom carries
Being toward Truth
Into the presence
Of The Unknown God.

Enduring the dull round
Allows the spirit
To follow Truth
Through the unknown
Onto forevermore.

So
Death is the question
And life is the answer.

As being toward Truth hungers
For blessed assurance
And time shifts into a moment
With The Spirit of Wisdom

The heart of what matters
Feels the always already there.

Then
Mind follows the language
Of being and nothingness
Until a sign from the beyond
Unearths hidden meaning.

It is
Pure music that wills
The deep touch
To liberate the despair
Of the here and now
From the constraints
Of the dull round
From the cage
Of linear time and space
As the breath
Of a vertical column of time
Fills the moment
With epiphany after epiphany.

Because
The shadows of self-deception
Sink into a sea of the abyss
Being toward Truth
Climbs out of self
As time present reflects
Truth pouring the authentic article
Into heart
Through a looking glass.

Pyramiding through what is there
Mind travels

Into the always already there
Where being and nothingness
Steps into silence.

Then
The voice of the wilds
Calls upon the light
Of the everlasting
And freedom carries
Being toward Truth into the presence
Of The Unknown God.

Enduring the dull round
Allows the spirit
To follow Truth
Through the unknown
Onto forevermore.

So
Death is the question
And life is the answer.

In the garden
Of tables and chairs
When the celestial clocks
Mark destiny
Lock N. Load takes to trance
A moment when a parabola
Of time
Opens a portal to Truth
While anchored
In phenomenal reality.

It is
That eternity is adopted
Into the presence
Of The Unknown God
As an outpouring
Of pure music liberates
Substance from darkness
As the mystery of life
Unfolds images of forevermore.

So
The dull round abuses Truth
With doublespeak
While the tribe guards
The language of what matters.

It is
A war between being
And nothingness
As Lock N. Load finds
The way, the Truth
And the life
While a vertical column of time
Shines upon the shadows
Of hidden meaning.

How
The struggle of the inside
Reflects the upheaval
Of the outside
As the world orbits
Self-deception.

Then
A thought wanders

Into the purpose
Of being and nothingness
As the existential moment
Drowns in the experiential.

So
In the garden
Of tables and chairs
Lock N. Load collects
The treasures
Of the deep touch
Believing the message
Of The Word.

Then
The Spirit of Wisdom
Embraces Lock N. Load
In the living moment.

From the grave of despair
Rises Truth
Through being and nothingness.

As meditation takes the moment
Where time and space configure
Another reality
Thoughts speak in images
And the deep touch
Reaches into mind.

There is
The inner eye in the center
Of being and nothingness

That signals the beginning
Of a parabola of time
As The Spirit of Wisdom
Eases into being toward Truth.

Then
The vision of The Word
Awakens blessed assurance
And heart feels the movement
Of things in themselves
Across the terrain
Of the here and now.

So
There were times
When nothingness brought despair
And mind
More broken than not
Spun wildly into the abyss.

So
The will to be
Brought the reflection
Of a presence
To being and time
As faith in The Word
Liberated what matters
From bondage
To the dull round.

Then
Pure music appears
In the language
Of the close at hand
As a portal to the beyond

Takes the senses
Onto a two-dimensional reality
And linear time and space
Anchor the substance
Of possibility.

What treasure it is
To ride the way
The Truth and the life
To pure music
As the wind speaks freedom
Into the presence
Of being toward Truth.

So
The mystery of life takes
Being toward Truth
Beyond the moment
And into the epiphany
Of all and everything
For forevermore.

Out from the shadows
The puppet masters schemed
To spread their lies
Onto an unprepared world
As their plague decimated
Nation after nation.

Although there was
The cry of the dying
That engulfed the globe
As a virus swept

The living into a shallow grave
Lock N. Load rallied the tribe
To dispense this evil.

How
The hunger for power
Led the puppet masters
Into a blood lust
The carnage scattered
In the streets
Of homeland after homeland.

No one was exempt
From this plague
All were victims.

Although the language of evil
Twisted the mind
Of the world
Olivia from oblivion
Lady liberty spoke Truth
Throughout the world
As the antidote
To the plague brewed
In the bastions of hope.

How
Many must perish
Until the Truth be known
As a new cold war
Covered the here and now.

So
Nations of liberty
Took the war

Of principalities
Into the light
Of what matters
And the struggle
For a free world
Allowed the tribe
To speak on behalf
Of Truth.

So
The people of the world
Banned together to outlaw
The puppet masters
Who were destined
To a tent of ashes.

To perceive things
In themselves
When looking at the close
At hand allows the reaching
Into the substance
Of what matters
As time and space
Conform to the rubric
Of a parabola of time
And to dwell
In a two-dimensional reality.

This knowledge enables
Lock N. Load to out-flank
The rhetoric
Of the puppet masters
With words that carry

The will of Truth.

How
The war of words
Pains the mind
While the plague
Destroys the flesh.

So
The tribe advances
The way, the Truth
And the life
Nourishing the spirit
Of the world
While the puppet masters
Want to control the world
By drowning Truth.

It is
That freedom relies
On the dissemination
Of Truth
Allowing trust to grow.

It is
That a world inflamed
With deception buries
The will of the people
As liberty and justice die.

So
Olivia from oblivion
As the life
Of lady liberty
Leads the tribe

To victory
Over the puppet masters
As Truth goes marching on.

So
The war of principalities
Ends with the light
Of Truth
Conquering the darkness
Of deception.

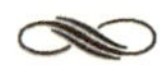

The strong will
That conquers injustice
Resides in the geometry
Of being toward Truth.

So
Lock N. Load launches
Truth into the logic
Of the puppet masters.

It is
Their agenda to peal reason
From life and confiscate purpose
Forcing the world to wander
In darkness.

How
Lock N. Load invaded their tent
Of deceit, pulling the trigger
On their lies
As the tribe vanquished
Their diabolical enterprise.

It is
That Truth is a gift
Of countless treasures
From The Unknown God.

It is
That Truth speaks
To the heart
In a language
Of dawning moments.

It is
That Truth fills
The void left
By the puppet masters.

So
Lock N. Load, an old warrior
Leads the charge
In the battle
Of principalities
With Olivia, the lady of liberty
Fostering the guns
Of a clear mind
And a pure heart.

So
The walls of division
Amassed by the puppet masters
To isolate the spirit
Crumbled into a land
Of waste
As the tribe took
The people into a world
Of the free and the brave.

How
Close the world was
To being trapped in a tyranny
Of hopeless slavery.

To read the substance
Of time and space
And to grasp
The underpinnings
Of what matters
Being toward Truth travels
With The Unknown God
Across the frontier
Of the here and now
And into the breath
Of being and nothingness.

Probing possibility
And the mystery of life
Allows the inner eye
To apprehend the purpose
Of it all
As mind unwinds
The celestial clocks.

It is
Through the unknown
That Truth rises
From the concealed
Into the existential moment
As the authentic article
Indwells the spirit
Of presence.

How
Blessed assurance
Endows the heart
With the approach
To The Word
As want and need
Feed the sheer will
Of being toward Truth.

So
Time past leaves
A trace to enlightenment
As time present
Sketches passion
For the way
The Truth and the life.

Although
It is a journey
Into the unknown
And the following
Of possibility
That allows being toward Truth
To live on with abundance
It is The Unknown God
That offers the peace
Beyond understanding
In time future.

During an interlude
When the war was far away
Lock N. Load embraced

Lady liberty with the passion
Of a hot summer night.

They were
Engaged in the deep touch
As their breath quickened
And time trumpeted
The climax of time and space.

How
The hours rolled
Into times and a half
As Lock N. Load
Tickled Olivia
And she danced
With full pleasure.

It was
The fragrance of love
That seduced the moment
As the sky looked on
In silence.

Then
The flow of pure music
Brought them together
The rhythm of love
Passing them
Into the drive for more.

Then
The drums of forever spoke Truth
To their being toward Truth
And a song followed them
With the desire in their blood.

Although
The interlude reached
Far into the beyond
With the will
To be together
The echoes of war
Broke their bones.

Eternity was a step away.

To live and love
With the treasures of their bond
They formed the substance
Of what matters
As they licked their wounds.

Then
It was back to the front lines
Where life ended
But love left echoes in their hearts.

Within the grasp
Of the wilds
Where the raw of eternity
Found the life of the living
Nonbeing marched
Through the unknown.

It was
The elucidation
Of time and space
That only the crow knew.

It was
The hidden meaning
Left by a trace
Of Truth
That led the crow
Onto the always
Already there.

Olivia from oblivion
As the countenance
Of lady liberty
Brought the vision
Of an existential moment
A seeing onto forevermore
And the following
Of the crow.

How
Truth shone ever so brightly
As Olivia purged
Nothingness from time
And times and a half.

Then
The calculus known
To the mystery of life
Figured the way
The Truth and the life
As the dawn of thought
Brought a portal
To the beyond.

Then
The image of pure music
Painted silence

To the here and now
As the heart felt the radiance
Of The Unknown God.

So
Nonbeing pyramided
Through the unknown
With the vision
Of the inner eye
Guiding being toward Truth
Onto a reality of Truth.

It was
The whole body of Truth
That allowed nonbeing
To be born outside
The blue of the world
Outside time and space.

Then epiphany.

SECTION 4

The orchestration of pure music

As the celestial clocks
Chimed the presence of the way
The Truth and the life
The Spirit of Wisdom
Pulled nonbeing
From being toward Truth.

It was
A passage through a looking glass
Into being and nothingness
Defining the existential moment
Revealed by the dep touch.

It was
Through the unknown
That allowed
Hidden meaning to surface
Bringing a vision
Of awesome grandeur.

Then
The experiential reflected
The look of a two
Dimensional reality
As nonbeing eclipsed
Time and space.

Although
Beneath the mask

Of self-deception
Lay a fragile form
There is the spirit
That desires
Blessed assurance.

Although
The war of principalities bleeds
Life from the living
The Word carries hope
Into the void of nothingness.

Then
A portal appears
In a two-dimensional reality
That leads to a vertical
Column of time
As The Spirit of Wisdom
Feeds nonbeing
With the mana
From forevermore.

To look beyond
Self-deception
And to share Truth
Nonbeing leaps
Into the substance
Of The Unknown God.

Then
The mission begins.

So
An old man raises his look
Into a starry night
Pyramiding the form
Of being and nothingness
As time and space
Yield to nonbeing.

He is in a trance
Spearheading the advance
Of the authentic article
Into thee dynamic
Of the here and now.

Then
Pure music fills the air
With the fragrance
Of an intoxicating mystery
And a portal
In the starry night
Gathers presence.

It is
That the old man
After decades
Has not outlived himself
But rather
He has expanded
His vision
With possibility.

For him, nothingness
Was of the impossible
In time present
As the substance

Of being toward Truth
Eclipsed time and times
And a half
As a crimson moon
Drifted across his heart.

While in trance
The old man visited
The unknown
Finding hidden meaning
In the looking glass
Of what matters.

So
The moment spoke
With thunder in its voice
And the old man listened
To the shadows
Of being and nothingness
Learning the language
Of the immediate.

Then
The Spirit of Wisdom
Lit the way
Onto the always
Already there
Through pure music.

So
She is the presence
Of lady liberty
Marching into war

A war between
Being and nothingness.

How
Her battle cry
Awakens life
As her maneuvers
Out-flank
The puppet masters.

It is
A time of when chaos
Rules the world
When a plague infects
The inhabitants
Of the here and now.

So
Olivia from oblivion
Assembles a tribe
Of warriors
To defeat those
Who hunger for power.

To preserve and protect
Freedom
Is their mission
As they advocate
The living Truth.

Then
The muscle of liberty
Grows in strength
As the tribe dresses
In the full armor

Of The Unknown God.

There is
No greater weapon
Than being armed
With Truth.

So
The war of principalities
Is one waged
On the inside and outside
Of being toward Truth
As mind seeks clarity
And heart seeks purity.

Then
Consumed by nothingness
The puppet masters rot
In a shallow grave
As lady liberty marches on.

In a universe
That has an infinite number
Of realities
There are only three dimensions
And the old man
Worked his way
Through the unknown
Probing what is there
With the deep touch.

So
Phenomenal reality

Is the inescapable rubric
Dwelling in the now
As the old man
Settles in the garden
Of tables and chairs
As the biological clock
Governs linear time and space.

Although to all
That has life
There is a beginning
A middle and an end
A before
A during and an after
But there are
Three types of time
In possibility
Linear time
Parabola of time
And a vertical column of time.

So
The old man employed
A parabola of time
As a transition
To frame time and space
And the celestial clocks
Govern this form of time
A time of two-dimensions.

The cosmic clock governs
The third type of time
A type of time
In a vertical column

Aligned with the cosmic clock.;
It has only one dimension.

So
From a vertical
Column of time
All and everything happens
All at once.

So
In the garden
Of tables and chairs
The old man
Pyramided himself
beyond being and nothingness
from being toward Truth
Onto nonbeing.

As time future
Redeems time future
Through faith in The Word
Nonbeing projects itself
Into pure music.

There is
Blessed assurance
In the dawn
Of phenomenal reality
That pyramids being toward Truth
Into the deep touch
Of The Unknown God.

Then
There is deliverance
From the dull round
Into the awesome wonder
Of a vertical column of time
Through a portal
In a two-dimensional reality.

How
Meditation allows passage
Into a moment
Beyond time and space
To the presence
Of The Spirit of Wisdom
As nonbeing searches
Through the unknown
For Truth.

There is
Hidden meaning
In the shadows
Of times and a half
That is of the authentic article
And nonbeing reads
The writing on the cave wall
To gather evidence
Of the way
The Truth and the life.

So
In the looking glass
Of a parabola of time
Nonbeing apprehends
Pure music
As a one-dimensional

Reality issues light
Into those shadows
Of hidden meaning.

Then
Nonbeing leaps
From the here and now
Into the hope that covers
Time past
As being toward Truth
Leaves time future
To the wind.

Then
The cosmic clock strikes enough.

From beyond
Came a smile
And an old man rose
Into a moment
When the deep touch
Wrote peace into his heart.

The struggle
Of decades of sweat
Broadened his horizon
Until Truth became
The close at hand
As he breathe in
The vapors of the always
Already there.

At his feet

Danced possibility
As the old man
Stepped into he other side
Of time and space.

It was there
In a parabola of time
That the war
Of principalities
Bloodied the earth
And the cry
Of the atrocity
Deafened the living of life.

Then
Nonbeing infused life
Into being toward Truth
As the old man called
Upon lady liberty
To gather the tribe
And prepare for victory.

As time passed
The tribe readied
For battle
As Lock N. Load reached
Into the canons of thought.

So
There was as plan
To combat the puppet masters
With the power of Truth
As the old man called
Upon The Spirit of Wisdom
Into the moment.

Then
The mask of self-deception
Worn by the puppet masters
Explode.

Then
The old man
Breathed in freedom
As lady liberty
Took the tribe into victory.

In the endless expanse
Of being and nothingness
Where the unknown
Grew into possibility
Lock N. Load gathered
Five smooth stones
Each a milestone
Toward the authentic article.

It was
His search for Truth
In hidden meaning
That brought him
To the edge
Of time and space
As the bells of eternity
Pyramided mind
Into the dawn of thought.

Then
The deep touch carried him
Through the looking glass

Onto a two-dimensional reality
As the celestial clocks
Projected him beyond the sky.

It was
That a portal rose
In a quadrant
Of time and space
Bringing Lock N. Load
Into a reality of pure music
And his heart echoed
The rhythm of the drums
In eternity.

How
The sound of trumpets
Announced the presence
Of The Word.

How
Hidden meaning formed
A destiny of hope
As Lock N. Load read
The drift of a one-
Dimensional reality.

Then
He leaped into the splendor
Of The Unknown God
As hidden meaning colored
Being and nothingness
With the blood
Of what mattered.

It was
A moment that brought
Possibility into the close at hand
As he figured the physics
Of the authentic article
And it was good.

In the wilds
Of the unknown
Thoughts connect to being
And nothingness
Through the experiential
As the inner eye probes
The other side
Of time and space.

It is
Through the here and now
That mind anchors nonbeing
Allowing a drift
Of things in themselves
To trumpet in the moment.

Accessing a two-
Dimensional reality
The old man sees
Through a looking glas
To gather what matters
As pure music pours
From the celestial clocks.

Then
A vision of time

And times and a half
Indwell the moment
With the deep touch
As nonbeing liberates
Life in the living.

So
Being toward Truth is
A process that moves
Toward Truth
After dislodging the mask
Of self-deception.

So
The confrontation
Of being and nothingness
Is the struggle
Of heart and mined
When the war of principalities
Inhabits the here and now.

So
The cosmic clock projects images
Of the always already there
From the glory and splendor
Of The Unknown God.

To be
At the front line
Of being and nothingness
Fixes an orbit
Around possibility
As the wilds
Of the unknown speaks
Eternity into what is there.

Then
Visions of pure music
Fill the old man
With the mystery of life.

From the here and now
The old man launches
Being toward Truth
Into endless possibility
As nonbeing gathers
The muscle of Truth.

There is
The coinciding
Of the biological clock
The celestial clocks
And the cosmic clock
That allows the old man
Access into things in themselves
And the beyond, simultaneously.

To be
At the threshold
Of being and nothingness
Where the war
Of principalities eats life
Nonbeing wears the full armor
Of The Unknown God
And is equipped
With the power
Of the deep touch.

Although
The puppet masters bleed
Life from the moment
The old man strikes
The language of self-deception
And time weathers
Their corruption.

There is
Strength in pure music
That overpowers
The puppet masters
Throwing them into a pit
Of darkness
As the will of being toward Truth
Secures the destiny
Of the old man.

Then
The trumpets sound
The advance of forevermore
As the deep touch
Liberates time
And times and a half.

So
The old man heeds
The call of The Word
As the language of Truth
Engages the always
Already there
As being toward Truth proceeds
Into the mystery of life.

So
Nonbeing knows life eternal
Through blessed assurance.

So
Olivia from oblivion
Known as lady liberty
Fought her way
Through the abyss
Where puppet masters
Held up.

She hooked up
With Lock N. Load
And together they led the tribe
From victory to victory.

They were warriors
And they were lovers
Bond together
Through the war
Of principalities.

Their walk of life
Transformed the dull round
Into a garden
Of tables and chairs
Where beauty and freedom
Thrived.

How
Their anthem brought
Pure music

Where cacophony
Of the puppet masters
Once dwelled.

It was
A victory for the tribe
As the troops liberated
Time and space
As Olivia waved
The star-spangled banner.

Then
It was time
To meditate on The Word
And lady liberty marched
Beyond phenomenal reality
Into a portal of Truth
As being toward Truth
Infused the moment
With a tribute
To The Unknown God.

Then
The Spirit of Wisdom flooded
The moment with visions
Of what matters
As the tribe followed
The call
To peace beyond understanding.

So
Lady liberty led
The battle to victory
Over the puppet masters

As freedom allowed
Being toward Truth to be.

So
Lady liberty is a warrior
Fighting for peace
And fighting for justice
As she dedicated herself
To freedom.

Grounded
In the here and now
She visits the stretches
Of time and space
Searching the unknown
For Truth.

How
Travels with The Unknown God
Equipped her with tried
And tested courage
As she faced those
Who hungered for power
Those who devoured freedom.

So
Lady liberty knew the ways
Of meditation
And she placed
Herself into trance
In search
Of hidden meaning

Finding the way
The Truth and the life.

It was
That she tapped
Into The Spirit of Wisdom
While she explored possibility
And she penetrated
The domain
Of being and nothingness
With the vision
Of the inner eye.

She knew
The river of thought
That flowed
With the deep touch
And she followed
The images
In the looking glass
Into realities beyond thought.

Placing her treasures
In eternity
Lady liberty learned
The grace and power
Of The Unknown God.

As she traveled
Through times and a half
She brought the light of Truth
Into the darkness
Of the dull round

Then
It was time
To enter trance
And to explore the unknown
To clarify
The mystery of life.

Being toward Truth stretched
The vision
Of things in themselves
From phenomenal reality
As trance took the moment
Into a parabola of time.

From that two
Dimensional reality
Emerged the beginning
Of nonbeing
As The Spirit of Wisdom
Issued the way
The Truth and the life.

It was
A passage into pure music
That trumpeted a portal
Into a one-dimensional reality
And being toward Truth
Launched mind into time
And times and a half.

Suddenly
Nonbeing opened
The inner eye
To times past
Where being and nothingness

Lived in the shadows
Of hidden meaning.

Suddenly
The geometry
Of time and space exploded
And the deep touch
Encompassed what was there.

Leaving the wilds
Of self-deception
Nonbeing thought itself
Into the light of forevermore
As min climbed
A ladder of faith.

Then
The Unknown God
Displayed the dynamic
Of what matters
As nonbeing faced
The smile
Of the everlasting.

Then
Chaos broke upon the scene
With a push from anarchists
And a nation throbbed with angst.

It was
A detachment
From the puppet masters
That triggered

A reckless abandonment
From Truth
As the heartless bled
Integrity into dust.

How
Darkness threatened
A land of liberty
And justice for all
As time passed
Into upheaval.

Then
Enough was enough.

It became
A war of hearts and minds
As the rising of a few
Threatened the freedom
Of a nation.

Then
An old man
Stepped into the light
Of Truth
Followed by lady liberty
And Lock N. Load.

He spoke
Truth into the horizons
Of time and space
Bringing life into the moment.

Then
Lock N. Load took

The star-spangled banner
Onto the front line
Of the war of principalities
And the puppet masters cringed.

Then
Lady liberty charged
The darkness
With the deep touch
And the power of Truth
Rained down
Upon the wicked
And the mindless.

So
The iron will
Of The Spirit of Wisdom
Brought freedom and peace
To the uprising.

So
It is pure music
That dwells in the heart
Of The Spirit of Wisdom
As a vertical column of time
Indwells all of time at once.

There is
No space in that time
As pure music blasts
Eternal light
Into the province
Of the here and now.

Although
The quick of being toward Truth
Recedes into the moment
Life fortifies nonbeing
With the spirit
Of the everlasting
As the rhythm
Of the eternal drums
Drives the will
Of what matters.

Then
The anthem
Of being and nothingness
Marches over self-deception
After surviving the war
Of principalities
And Truth becomes
The food of nonbeing.

It is
The will of to be
That steps into thoughts
Of possibility
As pure music
Elevates nonbeing
Into the celestial clocks.

Then
A parabola of time
Sings abundance
Into the moment
Carrying nonbeing
Beyond possibility
As time

And times and a half
Issue the light
Of The Unknown God.

So
Pure music births
The deep touch
Infusing love
Into the encompassing
As The Word trumpets
The here and now
Into the always already there.

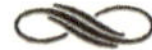

Submerged in pure music
Being toward Truth follows
The rhythm of the moon
Rising with the heart
Into times and a half
As nonbeing actualizes
In a two-dimensional reality.

It is
The projection from there
That liberates
Being and nothingness
From the prison
Of the dull round
As the secrets
In the here and now
Carry nonbeng
Into the province
Of endless possibility.

How
Mind marches to the edge
Of phenomenal reality
While heart fastens
To the unknown
Revealing the substance
Of what matters.

Then
Thought draws an idea
Beyond the quick
As life pours Truth
From the everlasting
As pure music delivers
The deep touch
To understanding.

Then
Wave upon waves of light
Pronounces the moon
Into the breath
Of beauty and wonder
As the sky opens
To a looking glass
Leading to the other side
Of the close at hand.

It is
That the trace
Of the moon
Presents echoes in the mind
As pure music elevates
The vision to Truth.

Then
Nonbeing unfolds hidden meaning
As an epiphany
Writes Truth into the heart.

So
Truth unites heart and mind
Through the echoes in trance.

Then
It was cut to the quick
By Lock N. Load and lady liberty
As the tribe charged
The domain
Of the puppet masters.

So
It was the language
Of hidden meaning
They attacked
To wipe out the age
Of deception.

Buried in the debris
Of nothingness
Truth gasped for air
As lady liberty drove
The muscle of a tongue
Designed for freedom.

Then
A dialogue proceeded
To unearth what matters

And the tribe followed
The echoes of time
And times and a half
Into a moment
With The Unknown God.

Upon the plane
Of a two-dimensional reality
Lady liberty brought
The deep touch
Into a valley of dried bones
As the dull round emerged
Into the light
Of The Word's presence
And the puppet masters
Scattered.

Breaking through the moment
Lady liberty danced
A dance of war
As pure music released
The power of cosmic
Consciousness and Truth
Emerged from the rubble.

So
It is that Truth speaks
With a language
All its own
As heart feels its way
Into the here and now.

How
The close at hand opened
To a celebration of spirit

As The Word penetrated
Things in themselves
With the certainty
Of pure music.

Thrown into the here and now
Being toward Truth stretches
Through time and space
Feeling the way
The Truth and the life.

As the look
Of the inner eye
Senses the beginning
Of a moment
Nonbeing awakens
To the substance
Of the beyond.

Then
Being and nothingness
As a singular presence
Probes the other side
Of eternity
Liberating being toward Truth
From the shadows
Of the dull round.

So
Being toward Truth
Is designed
To be toward Truth
While being there

Hides behind the mask
Of self-deception

It was
In the moment
That nonbeing
Delved into a parabola
Of time
As the celestial clocks
Chimed destiny into mind.

How thoughts followed
The dance of pure music
Onto horizon after horizon
Of the expanse triggered
A vision
Of pure music
The substance of the always
Already there.

Pulling out of trance
Nonbeing lettered
A language of Truth
And carved it
Into the heart
Of being toward Truth.

So
Nonbeing indwells
With the horizon
Of being toward Truth
As The Spirit of Wisdom
Fuels the mystery of life.

It was
A time when puppet masters
Pulled the trigger
Plunging the world into chaos
With bodies crawling
Into unmarked graves.

Staggering, the body count
Of the world
Caused nation after nation
To stumble
As time and spacer
Owned into disaster
And life fell into dust.

So
The puppet masters arranged
A plague that swept
Across the dull round
As they fed deceit
To the survivors.

It was
Those who hungered for power
That brought the collapse
Of freedom
As anarchy took to strongholds
In the streets.

It was
A time when lady liberty wept.

It was
A time when freedom fell
As the puppet masters

Inflicted anarchy
In the life
Of the star-spangled banner.

It was not
Peaceful demonstrations
That hung Truth.

It was
The deviance
Of Acorn that struck
The heart and mind
Of Truth.

Then
The tribe gathered
In the garden
Of tables and chairs
And Lock N. Load raised
The red, white, and blue.

So
A new war of principalities
Raged in the moment
But Truth had the power
Of blessed assurance.

It was
Time to engage
The monsters of destruction.

Victory is on the side of Truth.

So
The spirits of the dead
Marched out of their graves
And they were hungry
For justice.

It was
Dawn and Truth rose
With the sun
Bringing light
Of The Word
To a blind world
A blindness inflicted
By the puppet masters.

In a world
Where there is no Truth
The power mongers
Control the minds
Of the populace
Targeting free spirits.

Then
The star-spangled banner
Gathered in a fist
Of freedom
As the deep touch
Pyramided the faithful
Into the front lines
Of the war
Of principalities.

Blood flowed
Into a sea of madness
As lady liberty

Led the charge
Into a moment
Of times and a half
When precious life
Fought its way through death.

Then
The breath
Of The Unknown God
Infused the tribe
With the power
Of The Spirit of Wisdom
And the war seized the moment.

It was
A struggle for life
That brought down
The puppet masters
As the world
Gained the strength
Of Truth.

So
The domain
Of the power mongers
Dissolved in the blood
Of their iniquity.

∞

While in a one-
Dimensional reality
Lock N. Load visited
The treasures
Of the beyond.

It was
Breathing in
A vertical column of time
That brought him
Into the images
Of pure music
As all and everything
Pyramided nonbeing
Into being toward Truth.

With this vision
Lock N. Load opened
The moment
To blessed assurance
As being and nothingness
Rose into the presence
Of the deep touch
As a singular form
As The Unknown God.

Then
After stepping
Out of himself
Lock N. Load felt
The radiance
Of the other side
Of the looking glass
As The Word appeared
In triumph
Over the workings
Of the dull round.

There was
The movement of pure music

Unearthing the here and now
From its silent grave.

There was
The rhythm of the cosmic clock
That pronounced
The always already there
Into nonbeing.

Then
Lock N. Load learned
The language
Of what matters
And eternity advanced
Into his heart.

How
The drift of pure music
Carries Truth into mind
As the dynamic
Of the authentic article
Grows into being toward Truth.

Penetrating the ceiling
Of what is there
Nonbeing charges
Into a two-dimensional reality
To defy the workings
Of the puppet masters.

It is
With the celestial clocks
That mind proceeds

Through layer after layer
Of hidden meaning
As pure music
Reaches into being toward Truth
Through the will
Of The Spirit of Wisdom.

There is
The sound of images
Rubbing being into nothingness
As self follows the drift of things
In themselves into possibility.

Then
The Unknown God
Speaks nonbeing
Into the life
Of forevermore
As trumpets announce
The time and space
Of what is there.

Then
Leaving trance
The old man steps
Into the echoes
Of a vertical column of time
As the will of the age
Faces the chaos
Of puppet masters.

So
He recalls the Truth
Witnessed by nonbeing
In the valley of dry bones

And he takes
A hard line against
The puppet masters.

Then
Armed with the power
Of Truth
The old man targets
The chaos
And the language of chaos.

Although
The darkness hides Truth
Nonbeing lights
The way, the Truth
And the life through faith.

Looking into the interstices
Of time and space
Olivia from oblivion
Secured the dawn
Of what matters
As the substance
Of the here and now
Revealed the geometry
Of all and everything.

Then
The order of things
In themselves
Built an image
That spanned a vision
Of each reality

And The Spirit of Wisdom
Formed a looking glass
Into the unknown.

Focusing on thee deep touch
Olivia traveled
Into the unknown
Gathering hidden meaning
And filling mind
With the mystery of life.

So
The minute particular
Of the here and now
Granted access
To the calculus
Of nonbeing
As thought figured
The mathematics
Of Truth.

Then
Life pyramided
Into being and nothingness
As the essential figure
Of presence brought
Pure music into heart.

How the trumpet sounded.

How the drums of eternity struck
Rhythm into what was there.

How a voice carried a song
The anthem of forevermore.

Then
Olivia felt the beginning
Of a moment
With The Unknown God
As the blessed assurance
Took her into figures
Of things in themselves.

Then
She saw in the looking glass
The way, the Truth and the life.

Through her dance
With The Spirit of Wisdom
Lady liberty feels the muscle
Of pure music
As she moves ever so gracefully
Through a looking glass.

Once
On the other side
Of times and a half
She follows a river of Truth
Into the frontier
Of the unknown.

There is
Th quick of the drums
That surrounds her
As mind leans
Toward a one-
Dimensional reality.

Suddenly
The earth gives up
A body of Truth
And the sky glows
With the radiance
Of The Unknown God.

So
This here and now
Encompasses linear time
With the light of forevermore
Allowing lady liberty
To cleanse the wounds
Of battle.

In time
The juxtaposition
Of being and nothingness
Takes mind
Into the connectivity
Of the deep touch
And she leaps into time past
To recall the authentic article.

Lady liberty wears no mask
But cleanses the look
That speaks Truth.

Opening the wilderness
Of hidden meaning
She frees thoughts
Of possibility.

Then
The echoes of Truth

Take her
Into the peace beyond
Understanding.

To read
Inside time and space
Where the interstices
Of things in themselves
Bleed Truth
Olivia from oblivion
Detaches being for self
From nothingness
As the deep touch
Guides her into trance.

In that moment
Her inner eye receives
Images of pure music
And the light
From the always already there
Introduces her to nonbeing.

Then
She feels the presence
Of The Unknown God
Take her beside
Fresh blood
As trumpets pyramid her
Into the mystery of life.

To be there
Among the lights
Of forevermore

Where things in themselves
Birth the rush
Of linear time
How
Olivia bathes in the blood
Of the war of principalities
As she reaches
Through a looking glass.

There is
A rhythm of pure music
Healing that which was dying
As The Word pronounces
Eternity in the moment.

Then
An old man appears
At the end of a channel
And he spreads his wings
Toward the unknown
Soaring into time
And times and a half.

So
The linear belongs
To the biological clock
Where the illusion
Of beginning traces
Time into possibility.

Then
Blessed assurance
Fills Olivia
With the authentic article
As believing herself

Into a figure
Of the always already there.

So
She believes herself
Out of time past
And into time future
As she steadies her aim
In time present.

Then
Olivia as lady liberty
Carries a banner of Truth
Across a world of hatred
And the tribe follows her
Into battle.

It is
A struggle for being toward Truth
To face outliving self
As mind tends to collapse
But there is the calling
Onto destiny to endure
Through nothingness
Onto the treasures
Of the beyond.

How
The bones groan
While under duress
But the will of nonbeing
Provides the strength
To charge ahead.

Then
The Spirit of Wisdom
Offers the light of Truth
And Olivia climbs
Out of self.

It is
That the darkness of war
Chokes the breath
But the way, the Truth
And the life guides
Her onto victory
As she breathes in
Pure music.

So
The tribe equips itself
With the power
Of the deep touch
Advancing
Into the front lines
And the puppet masters
Feel overwhelmed
By the legions off Truth.

Then
To follow the calling
Presents itself
As the message
From the always
Already there
And lady liberty pyramids
The tribe into victory.

So
The will of Truth forms destiny.

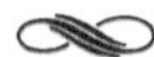

So
The mystery of life
Dwells in hidden meaning
And the inner eye
Follows traces
Of things in themselves
To Truth.

How
Pure music permeates
Times and a half
When being toward Truth
Reaches the deep touch
Transforming what is there
Into a walk
Around the moons
Of The Spirit of Wisdom.

Then
Nonbeing climbs
Out of self
Liberating a vision
Of thought
Beyond the here and now.

It was
An exploration
Of possibility
Through a looking glass
In a parabola of time

That allowed mind
To decipher the language
Of the mystery of life
As a two-dimensional reality
Framed a moment.

It was
Reading what was there
With the inner eye
That brought the image
Of the authentic article
Into view
As nonbeing anchored
In a parabola of time
And mind followed
The deep touch
Into a one-dimensional
Reality.

Then
Through a vertical
Column of time
All and everything surfaced
As a given
As a connection
To hidden meaning.

Then
The Unknown God
Granted blessed assurance
Through faith in The Word.

So
The mystery of life
Filled nonbeing with Truth.

So
There is the thing in itself
As phenomenal reality
And there is being for itself
As the given of man kind
But trance takes one
Into being beyond self.

It is
A mysterious wave
Of light and shadow
Dancing in the back of mind
As visions stir
From he deep touch.

Further into meditation
Takes thought
Into a looking glass
Where images speak
The language of pure music.

Then
Time and space dissolve
In the moment
Ass the inner eye follows
Being and nothingness
Into a two-dimensional reality
As the heart seeks
What matters.

Focused on the language
Of pure music
Being beyond self leaves

A world of hatred
And launches into the splendor
Of The Unknown God
To gather the strength
To endure.

How
It is to be in the world
But not of the world.

So
The spirit of being toward Truth
Registers the beyond
As a place of destiny
Where life lives in the moment
Of forevermore.

There is
The awesome wonder
Of The Word
That stretches the mined
To comprehend possibility
As the waves of eternity
Take nonbeing intro he rhythm
Of the always already there.

Without the deep touch
Of the beyond
Being for itself
Is destined to outlive self.

Then
The moment extends

Into times and a half
As a duration of nonbeing
Spreads its wings
Across eternity.

There is
A rumbling of thought
As the inner eye reads
The always already there
Finding Truth
In a valley of dry bones.

How
Things in themselves
Allow an anchor
A launching point
Into the beyond
As being toward Truth
Stretches the moment
Across possibility.

While traveling further
Into the unknown
Far beyond the here and now
Meditation feeds mind
With the deep touch
And the engine
Of The Unknown God
Drives nonbeing
Into an epiphany.

So
Olivia from oblivion reaches
Through a parabola of time
Into what is there

As a two-dimensional reality
And being toward Truth builds
A fortress of belief
Based on The Unknown God.

It is
That the foundation
Of all and everything
Is written in the physics
Of language
As mind follows
The echoes of thought
Into the deepest recesses
Of the existential moment.

Then
Lady liberty dismantles
The war of principalities
As the peace beyond understanding
Centers Truth
In the heart of the world.

Then
The puppet masters awake3n
To the folly of their endeavor.

Soon
Pure music will fill the world
With the way, the Truth and the life.

Seeking the language of treasures
An old man travels
Through the expanse

Of what is there
Challenged by the darkness
Overshadowing the here and now.

How
The rub of the deep touch
Awakens life
In old bones as mind focuses
Upon the living moment.

There is
Pure music in the passage
Into the unknown
That allows thought
To follow the traces
Of hidden meaning
And the old man
Gathers the light
From the way, the Truth
And the life.

Then
The trance carries him
Into an awesome wonder
Where Truth stands tall
And the mystery of life
Yields a vision
Of the always already there.

How
The labor of mind
Unearths the face
Of being toward Truth
As nonbeing conquers
The elements of destruction.

To tear down the wall
Of nothingness
The old man drives his fist
Through time and times
And a half
Until the will of nonbeing
Tramples the chaos
In a world of madness.

Then
The old man takes life
Into an encounter with darkness
And he pounds Truth
Into the debris
Of a lost world.

So
The language of treasures
Is the talk of the heart
With the pure music
Of The Unknown God.

So
Truth is the old man's legacy.

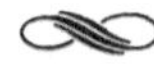

To experience pure music
How the marvels
Of the universe listen carefully
Learning the ways of wisdom.

So
The Phoenix and the bird
Of paradise are

A breeding pair
Their multitude filling the sky
With splendor
Their song captivating
All and everything.

Pure music is
A liberation of time and space
As the dynamic of Truth
Stirs hope into possibility.

Suddenly
The dagger of darkness
Penetrates the moment
Stabbing deep into the heart
Of what matters.

So
The testament of Truth
Shall not die but lives on
In the grace
Of The Unknown God.

Then
The blood of the age
Pours life into the living
As pure music transforms
Conflict into the peace
Beyond understanding
Through The Word.

Then
Pure music detaches
Being from nothingness
As an anthem

Of victory parades
Through time and space.

How the rhythm of pure music
Infuses Truth into the trance
Of a lifetime
As The Spirit of Wisdom deletes
The puppet masters.

So
The dance of freedom
Endures
Across each horizon
Of always and forever
With the rhythm
Of pure music.

The destiny of pure music
Is being with the always
Already there.

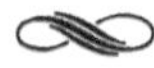

In the garden
Of tables and chairs
Olivia raised time
And times and a half
As she meditated on The Word
And she placed her mind
Into a wilderness of thought.

It was
Entrance into the deep touch
As a space
In a two-dimensional reality

Where the picture
Of all and everything
Took to being pure music
And lady liberty pyramided
Through the always already there.

Then
The celestial clocks
Moved the dull round
Out of the mystery of life
And Olivia built a thought
That encompassed
Being and nothingness.

So
The war out there
Echoed the conflict inside
And Olivia found understanding
Through nonbeing.

It was
Being toward Truth
That liberated her
From the bondage
To the puppet masters
As she wielded
The light of forevermore.

So
There was darkness inside
That mirrored the darkness
Out there as revolution erupted.

It was
The land of the free and brave

Against the power mongers
Against those drunk on power.

It was
That time when the tribe
Armed itself
As household after household
Stocked the shelves
With ammunition.

It was
Time to live for liberty
Or accept death.

As the conflict out there
Intensified
The war inside subsided.

As focus increases
On the war out there
The war inside turns
To peace of mind.

It is
That a sense
Of purpose gives focus
Focus on the war
Of principalities.

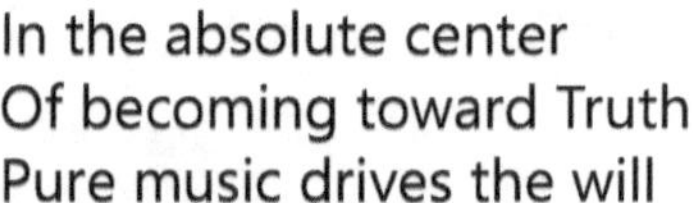

In the absolute center
Of becoming toward Truth
Pure music drives the will

Into a moment with the beyond
And nonbeing emerges
From a wilderness of thought.

Then
Heart draws the image
Of what matters
As a testament
To The Unknown God
And being toward Truth
Unravels the mystery of life.

So
In the mirror
Of times and a half
An old man gathers
The seeds of possibility
Planting them
In the mindscape.

There is
A rhythm to being toward Truth
That pure music teaches
As an existential moment
And the light of eternity
Embraces an old man
As he walks t the other side
Of being and nothingness.

Asa the experiential
Unwinds the celestial clocks
An old man accepts
The wilderness of thought
As the always already there

And he travels into the deep touch
Of the way
The Truth and the life.

So
The old man is the image
Of the quest for Truth
As he struggles
Through a two-dimensional reality
Until a doorway
To what matters opens
To forevermore.

How
He eclipses time and space
As part of his journey
Into the absolute center
Of being toward Truth
And he traces the rise
Of hidden meaning
Into the hourglass.

Then
The old man follows
The echoes of pure music
Into the splendor
Of The Unknown God.

In the balance of life and death
Is Truth
As a way to receive
The peace beyond understanding
And nonbeing dwells at the threshold

Of a one-dimensional reality
To gather the harvest
Of time and space.

To believe
In the way, the Truth
And the life
Unites mind and heart
With The Spirit of Wisdom
As the mystery of life
Liberates being toward Truth
From the dull round.

Then
Thought awakens the moment
When the inner eye
Perceives the horizons
Of possibility
As hidden meaning writes
Under the language
Of the here and now.

So
The figure of being and nothingness
Calculates the significance
Of the always already there.

How
The taste of freedom
Liberates dasein
From outliving self
As the doctrine of the mindscape
Establishes the route
To forevermore.

Then
The Word walks through the moment
When trance allows the inner eye
To see what matters.

Then
Mountains fall
Into a meadow of possibility
And Truth allows a vision
Of The Unknown God.

To accept
The always already there
As the promise
Of being toward Truth
Allows the portal
In a two-dimensional reality
To rise from the ashes
Of life and death.

So
The free spirits haunt
The puppet masters
In life and death.

When faith lives, death dies.

SECTION 5

Rubbing the beyond

In the quiet of twilight
When the world slows down
Mind follows the moon
Into the back side of time and space.

There is
The movement
Of the celestial clocks
Across the blood
Of the existential moment
As rivers of dreams
Flood thoughts
With images of eternity.

To reach
Into the breath
Of the always already there
Allows being toward Truth
To probe the unknown
As the close at hand
Anchors the advance.

Then
The milestones
In a two-dimensional reality
Mark the way
To Truth and life
As nonbeing orchestrates
The quiet of twilight.

So
Memories signal the presence
Of the deep touch
And mind leaps into the shadows
Cast by a hungry moon.

Then
Lady liberty binds her wounds
As Lock N. Load keeps watch
Over the perimeters of death.

Suddenly
It is dark
As the moon speaks
To the heart
And the metaphor
Of being toward Truth
Translates the language
Of darkness
Into the beginning
Of what matters.

It is
Out of the unknown
That births understanding
As the existential moment
Defines freedom as a right.

So
Lady liberty fills
What is there
With the deep touch
As The Word
Listens to hopes and dreams.

Then
Lock N. Load sinks into deep trance
As his inner eye
Sees the face
Of Olivia from oblivion.

She is lovely.

Ever deeper he sinks
Into the wonder of her face
As she issues the deep touch
And his body throbs
With delight.

To feel
The connection to the beyond
Olivia takes him
Into the warmth of paradise
As she surrounds
His form and substance
With passion.

So
It is moment
When he feels absolute Truth
And the thunder
Of The Spirit of Wisdom
Allows him to ease
Into pleasure.

Then
Olivia allows him to travel
To the other side

Of the experiential
As the deep touch causes him
To breathe ever so deeply.

Then
He enters looking glass
Finding the throttle of nonbeing
As he feels the titillation
Of the always already there.

Then
The sky opens to pure music
And Lock N. Load trembles
With passion.

So
The secrets of hidden meaning
Write upon his heart
As Olivia dances
In the flesh beside him
And the here and now
Sip into the unknown.

So
The trance takes him
Into her tender moments.

The seed has been planted
And from their faith
Grows the feel of eternity
As the world drowns in madness.

There is
The song of life
Weaving Truth in the heart
As passion rocks
The mind with cosmic
Consciousness
An old man breathes in
The sweet scent of forevermore.

Then
Being toward Truth sweeps
The shadows away
And the light of life
Connects him
To what maters
Aw the dull round explodes
With madness.

Awakening to the moment
Liberates an old man
From the constraints
Of the here and now
As nonbeing pyramids
Through the unknown
As he clarifies
Hidden meaning
And its cruel magic.

So
He walks
Through a looking glass
Taking with him
His faith
In The Unknown God
And his inner eye

Follows the rhythm
Of pure music.

Although chaos rules
The here and now
The old man welcomes
The peace beyond understanding
Into a vision of eternity.

Then
Real clock time disintegrates
As mind travels beyond
The unknown.

So these are the end times
As the plague devours
The children of promise
As the way
The Truth and the life
Returns.

The old man looks forward
To a thousand years of peace.

Upon a day of darkness
When tears melted the earth
Lady liberty stood her ground
Before the power mongers.

How
The fortitude of Truth
Sees the way
To victory over life and death.

As time and times and a half
Passed through the eye
Of a needle
Olivia took to Lock N. Load
And the world was never the same.

It was that their union embraced
The loving power of The Unknown God
And they, together, led
A nation of warriors.

Then
The day of darkness came
When the germ warfare hit
The world
And the world turned
Upside down.

Together
Lady liberty and Lock N. Load
Assembled the patriots
Into a mighty force
And the battle
Of principalities began.

There was
Blood on the city streets
As the carnage from thee plague
Piled across the land
And the world collapsed
Under the weight
Of the power mongers.

So
A nation of one tribe

And nations of Truth
Faced the pandemic
With a cure that stopped
The spread of the virus.

Then
Lady liberty raised the flag
Of Truth and justice
And the power mongers fell
Into ashes.

So
The minds of peace
Beyond understanding
Stand guard
As Truth and justice
Returns to the world.

The drama
Of political theatre
Smashes time present
As the will of power mongers
Eats life out of a nation.

As the hate of some
Throws a nation
Into an inferno
The cries of the innocent
Suffering in isolation
Eclipses times and a half.

Then
The clever are consumed

By their own folly
As the righteousness
Of lady liberty washes
The blaze away.

So
The swamp of stakeholders
Drains into the abyss
As the patriots determine
The destiny of a nation.

How
The deceptive schemes
Of the power mongers
Tried to cage the patriots
But Truth wills out.

They thought thee patriots
Were mindless cattle
To be driven into slaughter.

They did not anticipate
That the people
Would load their arms
Ready to defend their freedom
With a barrage of ballistics
As the patriots
Drew a line in the sand.

It was
A time when the enemy
Launched a plague
From the outside
While internally anarchists
Waged war against lady liberty.

So black lives matter.

So blue lives matter.

So lady liberty matters.

Then
Clever minds crumble
Into a wasteland
As their folly clogs their heart.

How
The morning of destruction
Awakens to end times
As the signs reveal
The destiny of life.

How
Long suffering lasts
Is kept by the celestial clocks
As the children of promise
Stagger under the oppression
Of clever minds
And the patriots arm themselves
With Truth and justice.

Feeling the closeness of death
Registers in the biological clock
And how a vertical column of time
Encompasses all and everything
With the love of The Unknown God.

So
Death has no dominion
Over the children of promise
As they fortify themselves
As they lock and load.

Then
The riders on the storm
Carry lady liberty
Into battle
Of a house divided
Against itself
And the patriots carry the banner
Of stars and stripes forever.

As the anarchists burn
The cities down
The children of promise
Ready themselves for civil war.

It is
That the children of promise
Believe in liberty and justice
For all.

So
The justice for the clever
Will be swift and complete.

Then
Olivia from oblivion
Meditated upon The Word
And the world fell into shadows.

As her trance
Proceeded into being
And nothingness
She felt the rise
Of the deep touch
And visions revealed
The rhythm of pure music.

It was
That the moment opened
A portal to the beyond
As time and space
Anchored her in the now
But mind felt its way
Far into the unknown.

There was
An epiphany
In the light of nonbeing
That lifted her inner eye
Into the peace
Beyond understanding
As a wilderness of thought
Dissolved the present.

Then
Clever minds tapped
Int the moment
And lady liberty armed
Herself For combat.

It was
That the thought policer
Were determined
To destroy all belief

And crush free spirits.

So
Lock N. Load and the patriots
Came to her side
And the battle began.

How
Cruel the magic
Of clever minds
That sought to destroy
The land of the free and brave
But the patriots formed
A multitude of defense.

So
It was revolution
In the streets
As blood flowed
Through times and a half
But lady liberty
Loved Truth more
Than she feared
Clever minds.

Armed with the passion
For freedom
Olivia headed out
To recover a nation
In distress.

On the road
She led a troupe

To a city
Being burned
By anarchists.

The troupe was a band
Of hardcore patriots who
Loved this country
And lived free
In a land of liberty.

It was
A time when all the stops
Were pulled out
When the police
Were hand cuffed
By corrupt politicians
But thee children of promise
Knew what freedom
Was all about
And they knew right
From wrong.

So
They road into town
With a soft voice
Not intending to start
Anything
But they knew enough
To be ready.

At nightfall
The anarchists continue
Their insurrection
Until the children of promise

Showed up.

Not a shot was fired.

So
The children of promise
\flexed their muscles
As their steel eyes
Penetrated the core
Of the anarchists
Cowards to the core
When faced by opposition.

After a while
The anarchists crept away
Leaving the life
Of the city to return.

So
Lady liberty gave the power
To the children of promise.

It was
That an old man
Stood at the brink
Of nothingness
As his trance
Took him into the substance
Of being toward Truth.

As nonbeing emerged
From the always already there
The old man set his sites

On the puppet masters
As the earth
Groaned for justice
And he gathered
The children of promise
To civil duty.

So
The children of promise
Were connected
To the way
The Truth and the life
And they were
Determined to uphold
Civil liberties.

How
The rhythm of pure music
Carried them
Into the domain
Of Truth and justice
As they readied
To liberate
The cities that burned.

It the blue lives
Did not put a stop
To the anarchists'
Insurrection
The children of promise
Would step in
And take care of business.

In no uncertain terms
The children of promise

Would win the war
Of principalities
With The Spirit of Wisdom
On their side.

Upon another front
Of the war
Was the plague
That more puppet masters
Inflicted upon the world.

How
The best and brightest minds
Attacked the plague
As the world staggered
Day by day.

There would be
Victory for the world
Because the children of promise
Held five smooth stones.

Slipping into trance
As the dull round
Vanishes in times and a half
Lock N. Load sought
Veritable reality
Of the mystery of life
As the possible showed
The face of what matters.

Then
The deep touch took him

Into pure music
As shadows of hidden meaning
Came into the light
Of the always already there.

As he proceeded
Into the unknown
Visions of eternity surrounded him
With blessed assurance
And the authentic article
Filled him
With the presence of life
As it is.

There were
Flashes of radiance in the warm
Of being toward Truth as nonbeing rose
Out of self.

Lock N. Load looked
Into the grave
Of outliving self
As he pyramided
Into thee other side
Of time and space.

There was
A treasure within the grasp
Through the looking glass
Of the beyond
And he reached for the heart of Truth.

It was the fortitude
Of this vision raised
Hi mind

Into a parabola of time
Where a portal appeared
That led
To The Spirit of Wisdom.

Then
The power of The Unknown God
Displayed a radiance
Through time and space
Upon boulevards of glory.

It was
The moment when Lock N. Load
Witnessed the birth of wisdom.

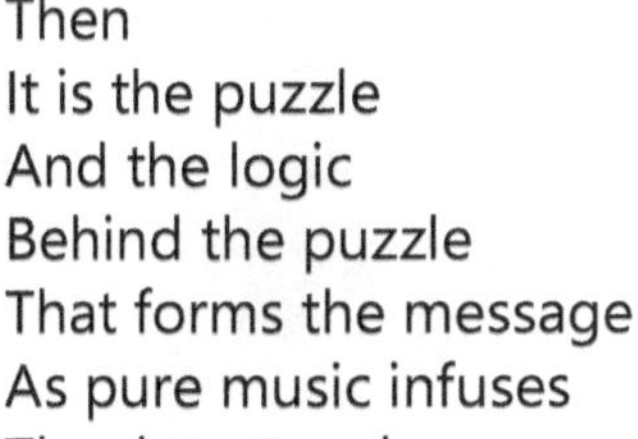

Then
It is the puzzle
And the logic
Behind the puzzle
That forms the message
As pure music infuses
The deep touch
Into the body of mind.

As becoming their approaches
Nothingness
The seeds planted long ago
Connect nonbeing
To The Unknown God.

So
Olivia measures
The boundaries of hidden meaning

From the inside out
As the dull round
Traces the path
Of things in themselves
Leaving behind the logic
Of the mystery of life.

To overlook
The rubric of being and nothingness
Rusts the mind
As the world grinds
What matters into dust.

Believing in the way
The Truth and the life
Olivia counters
The abominations in the now
As she steps outside
Phenomenal reality
Into the province
Of endless possibility.

How
The passage of linear time
Covers the bones of thought
But nonbeing presents
the mindscape
Into the always already there.

So
Lady liberty gave the world
Children of promise
The faithful to The Word
As Truth

Filled their hearts
As they lived
The puzzle and logic
Of the living moment.

∞

Among moments of Truth
An old man recalls
The beauty of a first love
And she, a treasure
Painted wondrous memories
Within his heart.

It was
A time when revolution
Was not in the wind
And the flag
Of live and let live
Flourished across the land.

How
Times changed
As anarchists pummeled
The stars and stripes
As the cancel movement
Uprooted Truth and justice
Burying history
In unmarked graves.

So
It became the duty
Of the children of promise
To account for times past
Because it is history

That enlightens
The mind of the now.

To live with the giants
Of times past opens
The door to the wisdom
Of the ages
Allowing mind to see
The working of Truth and justice.

So
The old man recalled
His own history
Placing I in the context
Of that moment
And he saw in the now
A movement
That had the desire
To destroy the splendor
Not only of his own age
But all ages.

What sadness it is
To deprive the world
Of Truth and justice
Revealed
In living history.

Then
The old man closed his eyes
And reflected
Upon the face of a true love
As he relived
Times of splendor.

While in trance
Lock N. Load saw
The mystery tree
Stained with blood.

It was
A time, long before
His time
That Love
Was nailed there
Upon a hill
Called Golgotha.

How
This vision poured Truth
Into his heart
As time and space
Hanged destiny.

Awakening to the now
Lock N. Load faced
The moment
When pure music
Was silenced
And he ached with the hope
Of deliverance.

Then
The world cried out
With apostasy
With the passion
To end all faith.

So
The plague crippled
The world
And the puppet masters
Danced with joy
But what they did not see
Was the power
Of the children of promise.

Howe
The children of promise
Were called
By The Unknown God
To take a stand
Against tyranny
And they were armed
With the way
The Truth and the life.

So
Lady liberty hunkered down
Facing those tyrants.

Squirming in their lies
The puppet masters
Crept back
To their infamy
Guarded by pure music
As Truth and justice
Pyramided the breath
Of freedom.

So
There were anarchists
Burning cities
Across the land
Of the free and brave
And in these cities
Murders and mayhem
Struck fear
In the hearts
Of those who lived there.

How
Even children fell from the gun shots
Of these domestic terrorists.

How
Twisted and corrupt
They were
Those who gave
No value to Truth.

So
There were three tiers
To the movement
To destroy this nation.

There were
The peaceful demonstrators
The anarchists
And the gangs
Woven into opposition
And each required
Its own treatment.

Then
There was
Germ warfare
Launched by foreign
Puppet masters.

As the devastation
Continued
Lady liberty formed
A strategy
To take care
Of the disturbance.

It was
In the stronghold
Of the children of promise
That a plan was developed
To return the nation
To normalcy on all fronts.

As time passed
And the plans executed
The Unknown God
Intervened
As an answer to prayer.

It is
One nation under God
Indivisible
With liberty and justice
For all.

It is
Stars and stripes forever.

SECTION 6

The End of Endgames

So
The war of principalities
Burned its way
Through life
As the puppet masters
Threw flames
Upon the home
Of the free and brave.

There was
Rampant disruption
Of law and order
As the puppet masters
Flexed their muscles
And the clever
Struck death
Upon lady liberty.

As they conducted
Mind control
They corrupted
A generation
With political correctness
Burying Truth
With the debris
Of toxic thought
But the spirit of freedom
Infused lady liberty

With the courage
To endure.

Then
Blood filled the streets
And chaos ruled the world.

Then
The darkness
Of the politically corrupt
Over shadowed
The way, the Truth
And the life
For a while.

Hanging in the wind
Were the dreams and hopes
Of the children of promise
Until the patriots
Armed themselves
With the bite
Of Truth and justice.

When faced with the power
Of the always already there
The puppet masters
Slinked back
Into their hole
Shaking in their filth.

So
In the end Truth wills out.

As cities burn
And the anarchists rage
Olivia from oblivion
Plunges a dagger
Into their mind
And their folly rushes
Into dust.

As the children of promise
Arm themselves
With guns of freedom
Lady liberty raises
The flag of stars and stripes.

There is
A spirit among the patriots
That faces the enemy
With a finger
On the trigger
And Truth in their heart.

Although the hate speech
Of the puppet masters
Feeds the anarchists
With encouragement
The children of promise
Nourish themselves
With the mana
From The Unknown God.

So
There is such a thing
As Truth
And there is such a thing
As freedom

While the puppet masers
Warp language
Twisting thought into a quagmire
Of deception.

Then
Time and times
And a half
Pass into the no longer
As the end times
Scatter living moments
Into the abyss.

Then
Truth infuses the world
With the peace
Beyond understanding
And a thousand years
Unfold with righteousness.

So
The destiny of the planet
Belongs to an epiphany
Of pure music.

Radiant
The song of the sun in times
And a half echoes
In the long of the light
As it awakens the inner eye
To nonbeing
And the drums of eternity

Strike a rhythm
In the heart of the world.

Treasures abound
Within the chambers
Of the living moment
As thoughts travel
Through the thick
Of what is there.

It is
That the light of forevermore brings
Truth to the table
As shadows of trepidation
Fade away
And the next fullness
Of time issues the peace
Beyond understanding.

Then
A message writes
Across the sky
With the signature
Of The Unknown God
And life begets life
From always already there.

There is
A sounding of prayers
And the world shouts out
Alleluia.

Then
The teaching of the way
The Truth and the life

Allows victory of life
Over death.

How
The children of promise
Populate the here and now
With thankful hearts
Because the narrow path leads
To Abrahams bosom.

So
It is true
In this life
That the hopes and dreams
Of the children of promise
Are fulfilled with the presence
Of Truth.

Then
The sun sets but the song
Continues through the everlasting.

Launching into trance
Olivia passed
The here and now
Add entered
A two-dimensional reality
Where the substance
Of being toward Truth
Found itself
Approaching nonbeing

Then
Time and space pyramided
Into the always
Already there
As she embraced
The engine
Of The Unknown God.

Once there
Olivia from oblivion
Opened her inner eye
And the trumpets
Of the everlasting
Awakened the moment
With blessed assurance.

So
Nothingness eclipses
Possibility
Until the seeking finds
The way
The Truth and the life.

Then
The deep touch fills
Olivia with the new teaching
And Truth exp0ands the mind
Into the peace
Beyond understanding.

How
The treasures from beyond
Enrich the moment
When presence dwells

In nonbeing
As the mystery of life
Yields to The Word.

Then
Olivia configures
Existential time and space
Into the narrow path
Leading to The Spirit of Wisdom
As the looking glass
Of the authentic article
Takes her into the given.

So
Through a leap of faith
Olivia feeds upon the manna
Of Truth.

It was
The language
Of the always already there
That brought
An epiphany of time and space
As an old man wrote
Across being toward Truth
With the blood of tyrants.

There was
A hymn of triumph
Spreading Truth
Across the landscape
While the folly
Of puppet masters

Plunged the world
Into chaos.

Then
An old man erased those
Who hungered for power
As he built a coalition
Of children of promise
And he fortified life
With the prayers
To The Unknown God.

Following the flow
Of pure music
The old man
Witnessed lady liberty break
The chains f mind control
As the world awoke
To the peace beyond
Understanding.

Then
The shadow of death
Reared its head
Connecting life
To living moments
And the old man knelt
Before The Word
Carrying the faith in Truth.

He did not turn his back
On life but faced death
Eye to eye
As his mission
Was not yet complete.

Surrounded
By veritable reality
He carved the beginning
Of end times
Into the language
Of being and nothingness
As space and time
Grew into the majesty
Of forevermore.

Then
The substance
Of what matters
Read Truth
Into the heart
Of being toward Truth.

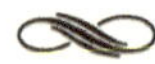

As an old man
Walked through the wilds
Of heart
The rhythm of ancient drums
Spoke the moment
Into living history.

It was
That all this life
Echoed in his steps
Into the unknown
As figures
From the other side
Of the experiential
Counted his breaths.

Out of no where
Came the call of a crow
And it wore
The face of being
And nothingness.

Speaking in the togues
Of apocalypse
The crow opened
Times and a half
To a fullness of time
And the old man
Bled thoughts
From his heart.

Then
Pure music emerged
From the moment
While the puppet masters
Rewrote history.

Then
The war between Truth
And double speak burned
In a valley of dry bones
And the old man
Took arms to the fight.

The way the he saw it
He had to crush
The serpents head.

Riding the quick
Of pure music
He felt the drums pummel

The always already there
Into the moment
And the children of promise
Followed lady liberty
Into battle.

Then
The earth bled with revolution.

Voiding freedom
Violating life, liberty
And the pursuit of happiness
The cancel movement
Took hold of the cities
And the children of promise
Were forced into submission.

So all of history was canceled.

So
They erased all of time past
Robed a nation
Of time future
And beat time present
Into submission
But the patriots
Drew a line in the sand
Waiting for the right moment.

The moment is now.

Up from the shadows
Rose the light

Of Truth and justice
As the patriots took aim
At the anarchists.

With thunder
In their muscle
The patriots took their stand
And the cancel movement
Trembled
Spewing out their guts
Into cisterns
Of degradation.

The children of promise
Armed themselves
With enough fire power
To take down
Those who tore down
A more perfect union.

Then
Lady liberty finished
The cancel movement
Returning Truth
To its rightful place
In the universe
Of pure music.

So
It was a lesson
Taught by tongues
Of freedom
As strength returned
To the muscle
Of law and order.

Then
It was time
To lock and load
And hit the road
To freedom.

Following the flight
Of the crow
Lady liberty transformed
Time and space
Into endless possibility
As darkness approached.

Then
It was night
And the anarchists
Took to the streets
Rioting and burning
The way
Into cancelling life
As it was known.

Staggering the world
The plague ripped
Life from the living
As the war of principalities
Both domestic and foreign
Attacked the world-wide
Children of promise.

Enough was enough.

When
The world-wide
Children of promise
Readied the game
With fists of fire
The anarchists scattered.

When the source
Of the plague faced
The world
Their tyranny fell
And the children of promise
Gained freedom.

How
Powerful the way
The Truth and the life
As The Unknown God
Forged the destiny
Of the puppet masters.

When
Olivia from oblivion
Led the children of promise
Into battle
The power mongers
Both domestic and foreign
Leaped into unmarked graves.

Then
The anthem of freedom
Became pure music
And the madness
Of the world died.

So
There are two aspects
To the mystery of life:
Life and death.

While living
There are thoughts and feelings.

Once dead
There are no thoughts or feelings.

So
These are thoughts
And not provable
Because once dead
Is an aspect
Belonging to the unknown.

So
One speculates about being dead.

Some believed
That once entered
Into the dead
There is nothing
And this may be true
But there is another idea
When there is a second death
When one is resurrected
And judged.

Destiny writes
That one is in either joy

And wonder
Forevermore belonging
To the side of Abraham
Or one is tossed
Into a lake of fire
For eternity
As a consequence
Of unbelief
And one's life activities.

So
He is the bed side
Of his love
As she approaches
The gates of the dead
And he is burdened
By his grief.

How
Grief is an encompassing
When all there is
Are tears bleeding
The heart dry.

How
He wants to believe
That paradise is her destiny
And that her pain
And suffering will end.

What cruel joke
This thing called grief.

After times and a half
He celebrates her life
With beautiful memories.

So
In the beginning
The Unknown God
Created time and space.

So
There is being
Rather than nothingness
As language defines
The size of the universe
As if it is smaller than
All and everything.

So
Infinity is on
A parabola
A two-dimensional reality
And parallel lines
Of time and space
Meet in endless possibility.

So
Entropy is a law
Of the linear
But The Unknown God
Is beyond entropy
And beyond the linear
As being
With a vertical column

Of time and space
As being omniscient.

So
As a figure
Beyond the linear
The Unknown God
Created entropy.

So
In the beginning
The Unknown God
Created the laws
Of physics.

So
Facts lead to evidence
And evidence leads
To judgement
But it takes
A leap of faith
To arrive at Truth.

So
In the beginning
The Unknown God
Created Truth
As the rubric
Of hidden meaning
As an element
Of endless possibility.

So
The games of mind
Probe the unknown

To grasp hidden meaning
Through pure music.

So
One of the purposes
Of Genesis 1:1
Is to identify
The Unknown God
As Creator.

In the hollow of mind
Thoughts had crumbled
Into dust.

A phantom violated
The workings
Of what matters
Leading the way
To corrupt
Being toward Truth.

It was a vicious assault.

Unleashing the lightning
Of justice
Eagle Hawk took on
The phantom
That killed Truth.

Following the stars
Through the celestial clocks
Eagle Hawk shook off
The poison in his mind

Putting his trust
In The Unknown God
And his 45 magnum.

With his gun blazing
He entered
A room of deception
And bodies fell.

From the shadows
Came a fist and a rage
Of fire struck home.

Then
Eagle Hawk, armed
With The Spirit of Wisdom
Took the moment
Into a two-dimensional reality
And thunder crossed the horizon.

It was
A battle of principalities
Where the viability
Of being toward Truth
Was at stake.

In this dimension
Eagle Hawk painted Truth
And the power
Wielded
By The Unknown God
Resounded across the world.

Then
The snake of this world

Was thrown
Into the lake of fire
A place of no escape.

So
The children of promise
Rejoiced
In their blessed assurance.